I0426223

NOTICE

This document is disseminated under the sponsorship of the U.S. Department of Transportation in the interest of information exchange. The United States Government assumes no liability for the contents thereof.

————————

This publication and all Office of Aerospace Medicine technical reports are available in full-text from the Civil Aerospace Medical Institute's publications Web site:
www.faa.gov/go/oamtechreports

1. Report No. DOT/FAA/AM-13/2	2. Government Accession No.	3. Recipient's Catalog No.
4. Title and Subtitle 2011 Aerospace Medical Certification Statistical Handbook		5. Report Date January 2013
		6. Performing Organization Code
7. Author(s) Skaggs VJ, Norris AI, Johnson R		8. Performing Organization Report No.
9. Performing Organization Name and Address FAA Civil Aerospace Medical Institute P.O. Box 25082 Oklahoma City, OK 73125		10. Work Unit No. (TRAIS)
		11. Contract or Grant No.
12. Sponsoring Agency name and Address Office of Aerospace Medicine Federal Aviation Administration 800 Independence Ave., S.W. Washington, DC 20591		13. Type of Report and Period Covered
		14. Sponsoring Agency Code

15. Supplemental Notes

16. Abstract

Introduction. The annual Aerospace Medical Certification Statistical Handbook reports descriptive characteristics of all active U.S. civil aviation airmen and the aviation medical examiners (AMEs) that perform the required medical examinations. The 2011 annual handbook documents the most recent and most widely relevant data on active civil aviation airmen and AMEs.

Methods. Medical certification records from 2006-2011 were selected from the Document Imaging Workflow System (DIWS), which is the FAA medical certification database. All medical data were abstracted from the most recent medical examinations with the exception of medical conditions which were historical and current. Only those with a non-expired medical certificate remained in the dataset.

AME records were selected from the Aviation Medical Examiner Information System (AMEIS). The current status of each AME was determined for each year of the study period from 2009-2011, retaining only those with an active status.

Airman variables include age, issued and effective medical classes, height, weight, BMI, gender, select medical conditions, special issuances, and FAA region of residence. AME variables include AME type, age, gender, medical specialty, pilot license status, senior examiner status, and region.

Results. Airmen: As of December 31, 2011, there were 594,912 medically certified airmen age 16 and older, and 32.0%, 21.8%, and 46.2% were issued a Class 1, Class 2, and Class 3 medical certificate, respectively. Across all medical classes, the average age was 42.7 years, and 93.4% of the airmen were male. The mean BMI for both females and males was 24.2 and 27.2, respectively. Seven percent of issued certificates required a special issuance. The most commonly reported medical condition was hypertension with medication at 11.1%.

AMEs: Of the 3,474 active AMEs, 94.2% were civilian, 2.2% federal, and 3.6% military. Nearly 50% reported their medical specialty as family practice. Their average age was 59.9 years; the majority (52.2%) did not hold a pilot license, and 81.8% were male.

Summary. This report contains widely requested data on the active U.S. civil airman population. This report is updated annually and is used by the aerospace community, including FAA leadership, aerospace researchers, advocacy groups, legislative staff, and the general public.

17. Key Words Pilot Medical Certification, Pilot Demographics, Pilot Medical Conditions, Pilot Statistics, Aviation Medical Examiners		18. Distribution Statement Document is available to the public through the Internet: www.faa.gov/go/oamtechreports	
19. Security Classif. (of this report) Unclassified	20. Security Classif. (of this page) Unclassified	21. No. of Pages 44	22. Price

Form DOT F 1700.7 (8-72) Reproduction of completed page authorized

CONTENTS

CONTENTS (continued)

FOREWORD

2011 Aerospace Medical Certification Statistical Handbook

INTRODUCTION

The annual Aerospace Medical Certification Statistical Handbook reports descriptive characteristics of all active U.S. civil aviation airmen and the aviation medical examiners (AMEs) that perform the required medical examinations. The 2011 annual handbook documents the most recent and most widely relevant data on active civil aviation airmen and AMEs.

METHODS

Medical certification records from 2006-2011 were selected from the Document Imaging Workflow System (DIWS), which is the FAA medical certification database. All medical data were abstracted from the most recent medical examinations with the exception of medical conditions which were historical and current. Only those with a non-expired medical certificate remained in the dataset.

AME records were selected from the Aviation Medical Examiner Information System (AMEIS). The current status of each AME was determined for each year of the study period from 2009-2011, retaining only those with an active status.

Airman variables include age, issued and effective medical classes, height, weight, BMI, gender, select medical conditions, special issuances, and FAA region of residence. AME variables include AME type, age, gender, medical specialty, pilot license status, senior examiner status, and region.

RESULTS

Airmen: As of December 31, 2011, there were 594,912 medically certified airmen age 16 and older, and 32.0%, 21.8%, and 46.2% were issued a Class 1, Class 2, and Class 3 medical certificate, respectively. Across all medical classes, the average age was 42.7 years and 93.4% of the airmen were male. The mean BMI for both females and males was 24.2 and 27.2 respectively. Seven percent of issued certificates required a special issuance. The most commonly reported medical condition was hypertension with medication at 11.1%.

Aviation medical examiners: Of the 3,474 active AMEs, 94.2% were civilian, 2.2% federal, and 3.6% military. Nearly 50% reported their medical specialty as family practice. Their average age was 59.9 years; the majority (52.2%) did not hold a pilot license, and 81.8% were male.

SUMMARY

This report contains widely requested data on the active U.S. civil airman population. This report is updated annually and is used by the aerospace community, including FAA leadership, aerospace researchers, advocacy groups, legislative staff, and the general public.

SECTION I. AVIATION MEDICAL EXAMINERS

This section characterizes the aviation medical examiners during 2011 with some comparative data from 2009 and 2010. All analyses represent data through December 31, 2011 unless otherwise noted. Data may slightly fluctuate annually from systematic changes and corrections to the records.

An aviation medical examiner (AME) is a physician authorized by the Federal Aviation Administration (FAA) to perform airmen physical examinations for issuance of FAA medical certificates. These physicians are designated according to the geographical distribution of airmen. There are also military facilities (installations) designated to perform FAA airmen examinations of military personnel for issuance of second- and third-class certificates.

AME seminars are held in each region and at Oklahoma City's Civil Aerospace Medical Institute to acquaint these physicians with the regulations and procedures governing the issuance of FAA medical certificates.

Table 1. FAA Aviation Medical Examiners by Year and Type

AME Type	2009 Number (Percent of Total)	2010 Number (Percent of Total)	2011 Number (Percent of Total)
Civilian	3,351 (93.8)	3,400 (93.1)	3,274 (94.2)
Federal	80 (2.2)	85 (2.3)	76 (2.2)
Military	140 (3.9)	166 (4.6)	124 (3.6)
Total	3,571	3,651	3,474

Table 2. Designated FAA Aviation Medical Examiners by Year and Region

Region	Newly Appointed Number (Percent of Total by Year)			All Active Number (Percent of Total by Year)		
	2009	2010	2011	2009	2010	2011
Alaskan	3 (2.1)	3 (2.0)	1 (0.8)	66 (1.9)	68 (1.9)	65 (1.9)
Central	8 (5.6)	10 (6.8)	2 (1.6)	184 (5.2)	186 (5.1)	176 (5.1)
Eastern	6 (4.2)	8 (5.4)	2 (1.6)	391 (11.0)	389 (10.7)	377 (10.9)
Federal/Official	7 (4.9)	4 (2.7)	3 (2.5)	102 (2.9)	109 (3.0)	98 (2.8)
Great Lakes	15 (10.5)	13 (8.8)	13 (10.7)	516 (14.5)	514 (14.1)	492 (14.2)
International	13 (9.1)	21 (14.3)	25 (20.5)	295 (8.3)	314 (8.6)	319 (9.2)
Military	31 (21.7)	27 (18.4)	25 (20.5)	130 (3.6)	159 (4.4)	114 (3.3)
New England	6 (4.2)	7 (4.8)	2 (1.6)	112 (3.1)	118 (3.2)	117 (3.4)
Northwest Mountain	12 (8.4)	11 (7.5)	12 (9.8)	359 (10.1)	359 (9.8)	345 (9.9)
Southern	17 (11.9)	17 (11.6)	14 (11.5)	702 (19.7)	712 (19.5)	678 (19.5)
Southwest	20 (14.0)	16 (10.9)	20 (16.4)	421 (11.8)	423 (11.6)	412 (11.9)
Western-Pacific	5 (3.5)	10 (6.8)	3 (2.5)	293 (8.2)	300 (8.2)	281 (8.1)
Total	143	147	122	3571	3651	3474

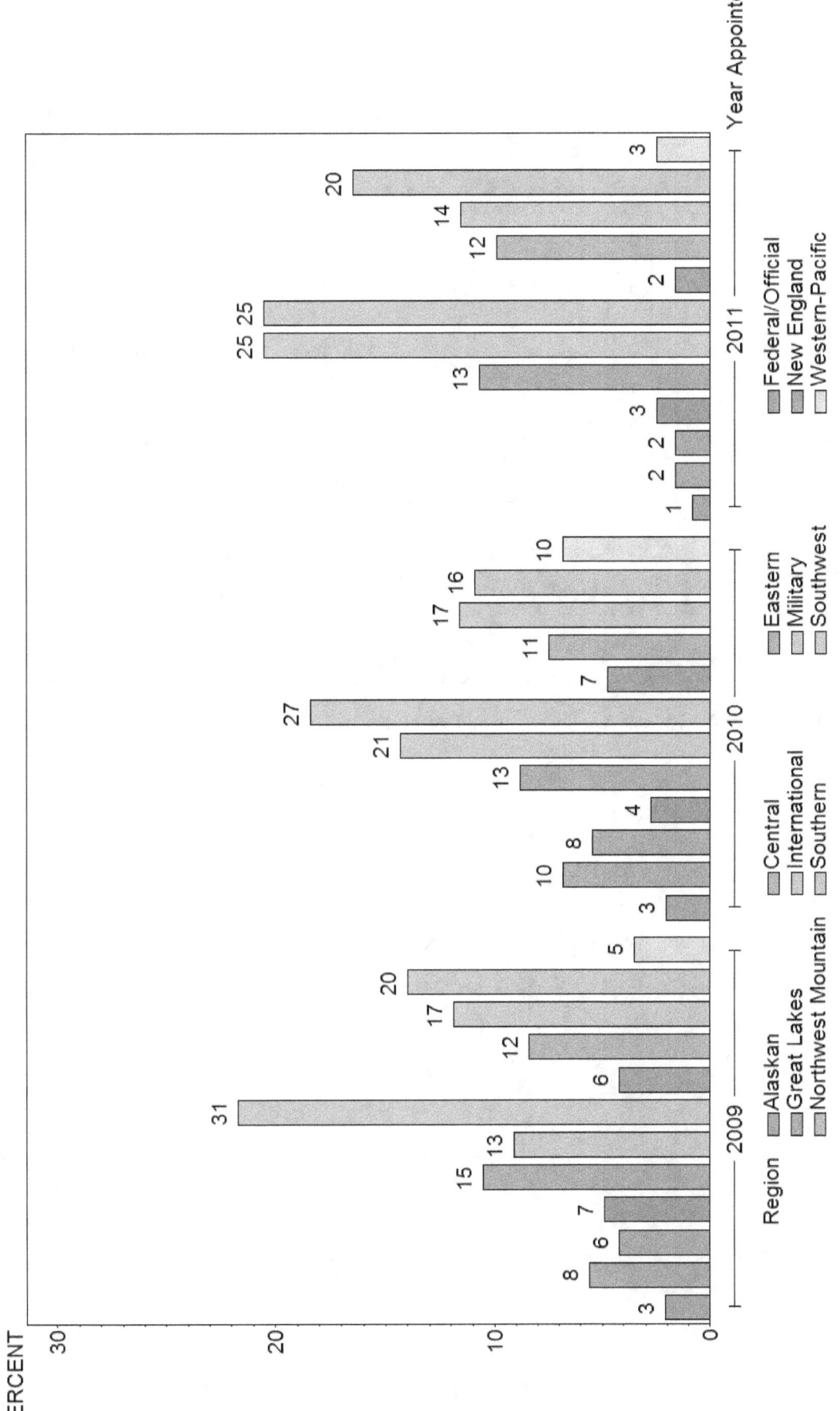

Figure 1. Distribution of Newly Appointed FAA Aviation Medical Examiners by Region and Year

3

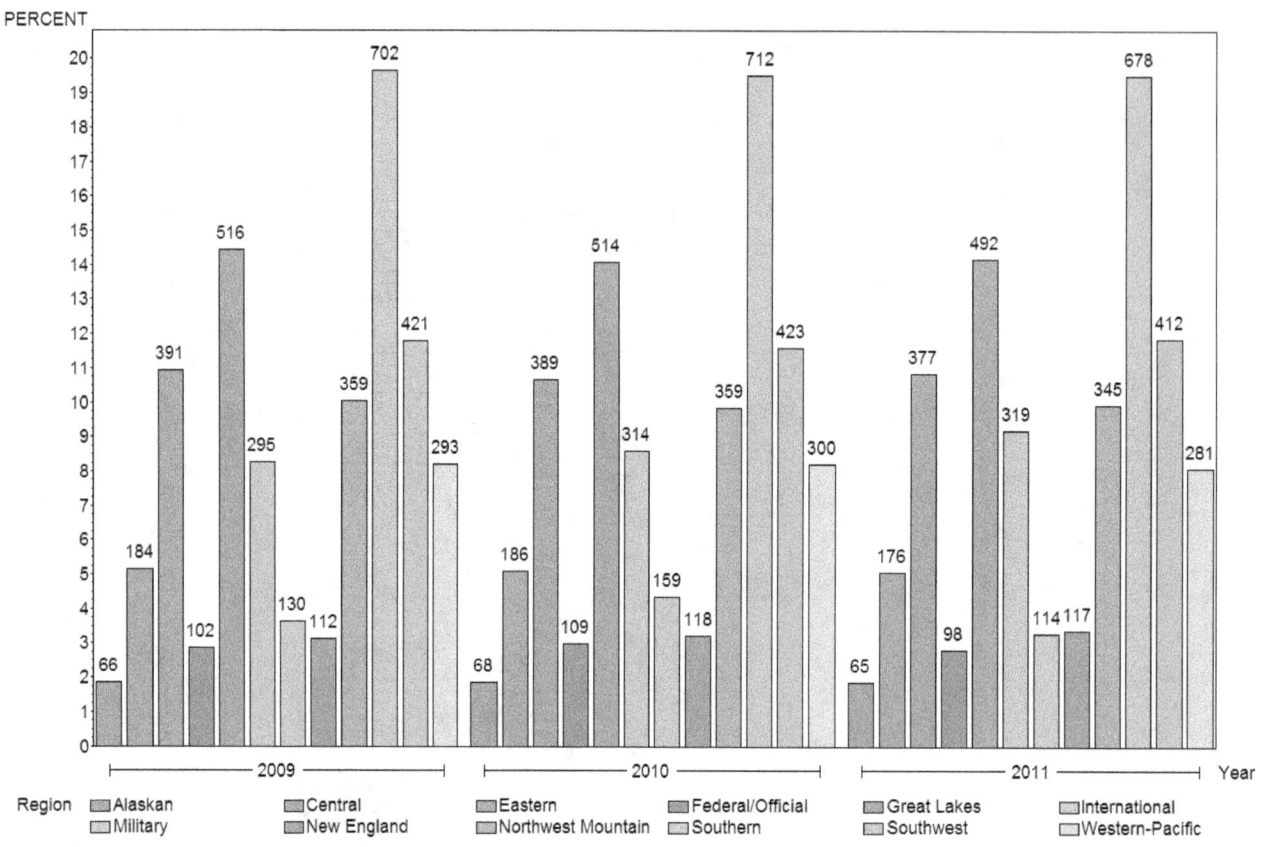

Figure 2. Distribution of Active FAA Aviation Medical Examiners by Region and Year

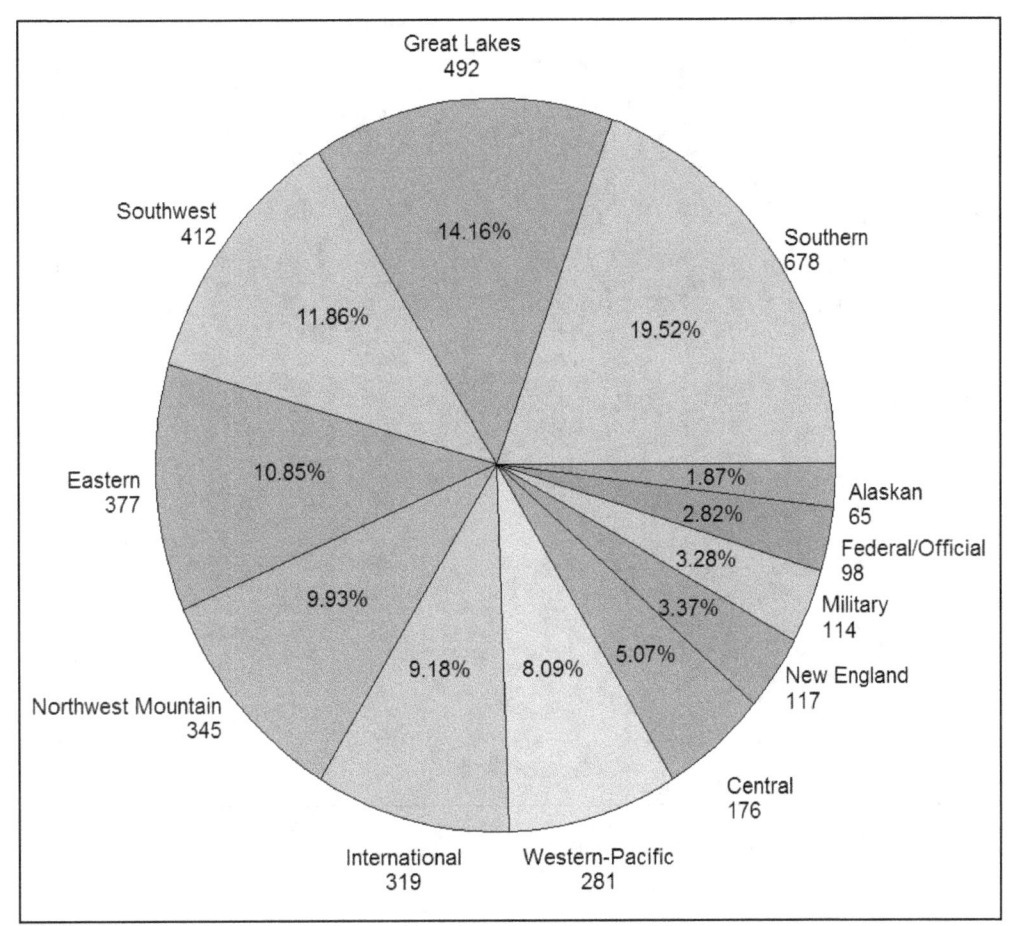

Figure 3. Distribution of Active FAA Aviation Medical Examiners by Region

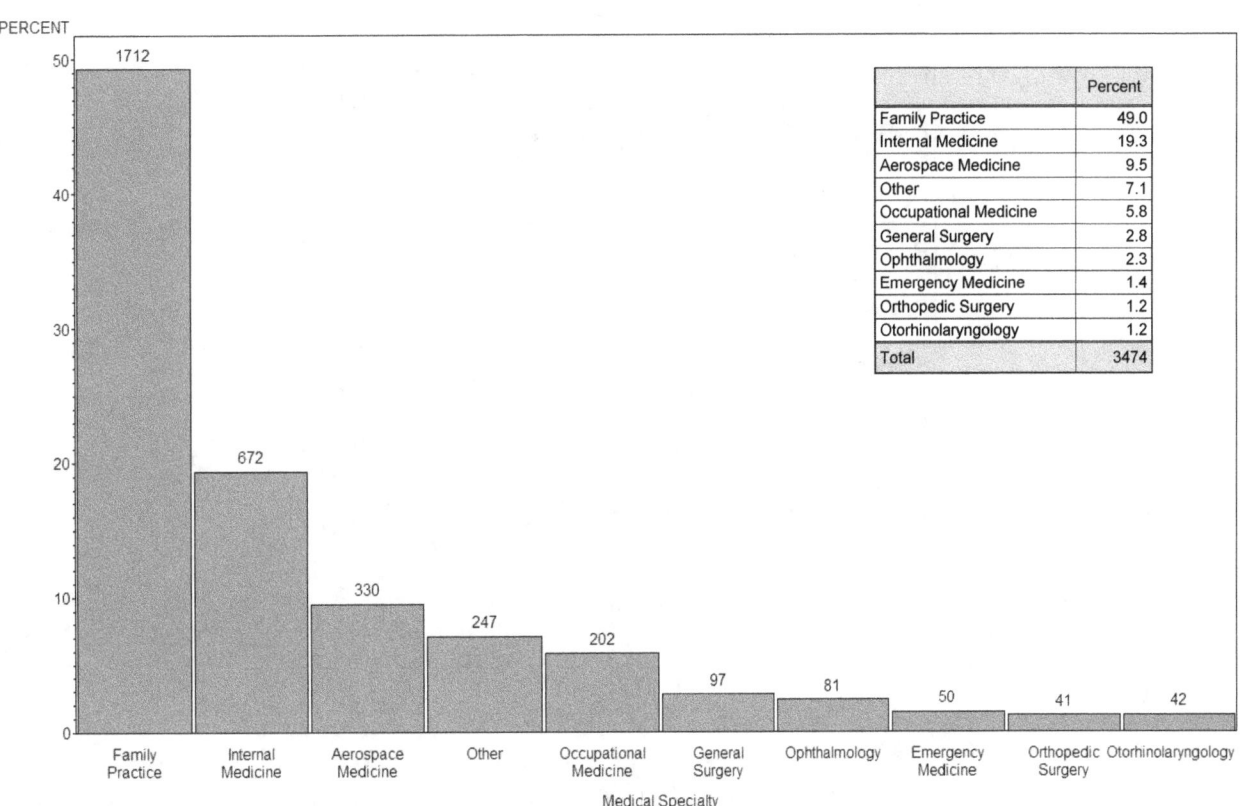

	Percent
Family Practice	49.0
Internal Medicine	19.3
Aerospace Medicine	9.5
Other	7.1
Occupational Medicine	5.8
General Surgery	2.8
Ophthalmology	2.3
Emergency Medicine	1.4
Orthopedic Surgery	1.2
Otorhinolaryngology	1.2
Total	3474

Figure 4. Medical Practice Specialty of Active FAA Aviation Medical Examiners

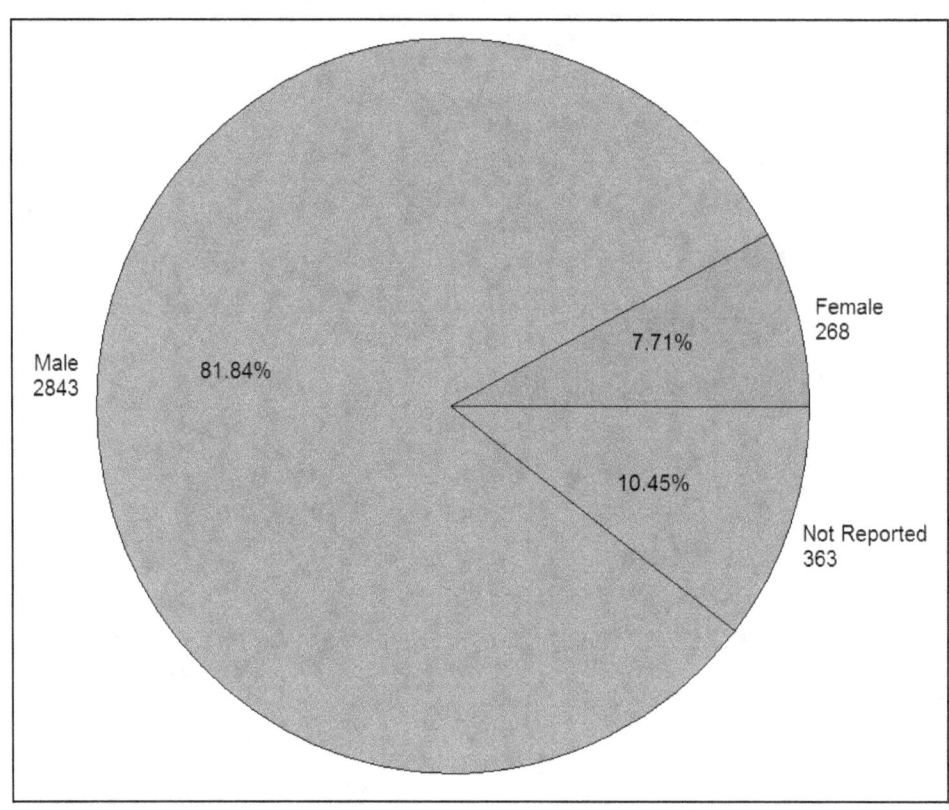

Figure 5. Gender Distribution of Active FAA Aviation Medical Examiners

Table 3. Pilot License Type of Active Aviation Medical Examiners

Pilot License Type	Number (Percent)
Commercial – Instrument Flight Rules	162 (4.7)
Commercial	87 (2.5)
Private – Instrument Flight Rules	134 (3.9)
Private	1102 (31.7)
Student	137 (3.9)
Other	40 (1.2)
None	1812 (52.2)
Total	3474

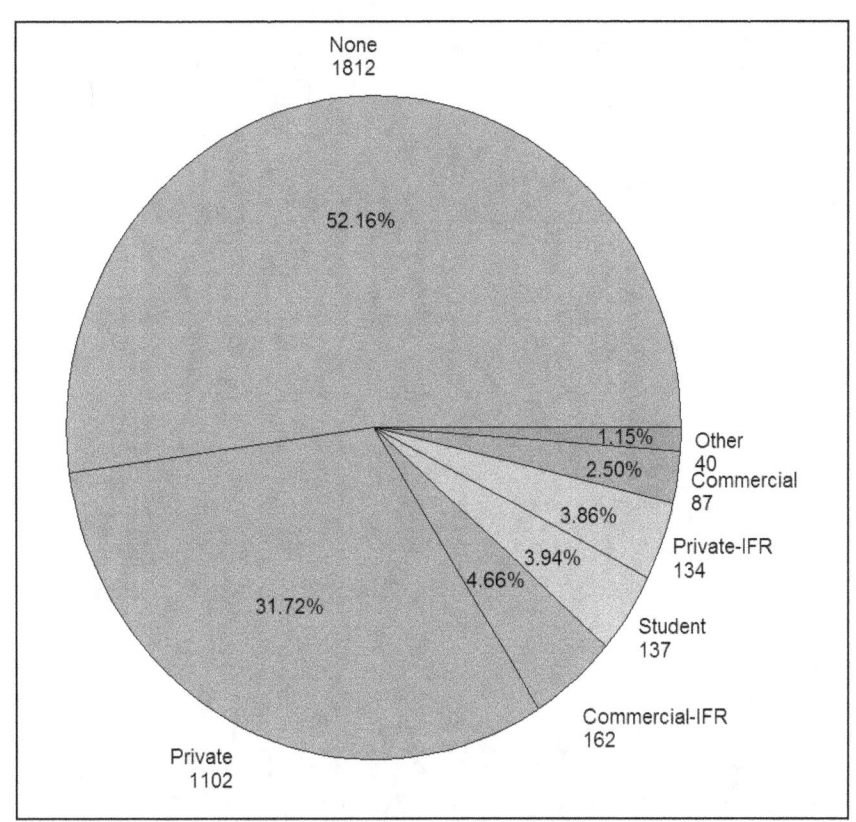

Figure 6. Pilot License Type of Active FAA Aviation Medical Examiners

Table 4. Senior Examiner Status of
Active Aviation Medical Examiners

Senior Examiner	Number (Percent)
Yes	2123 (61.1)
No	1351 (38.9)
Total	3474

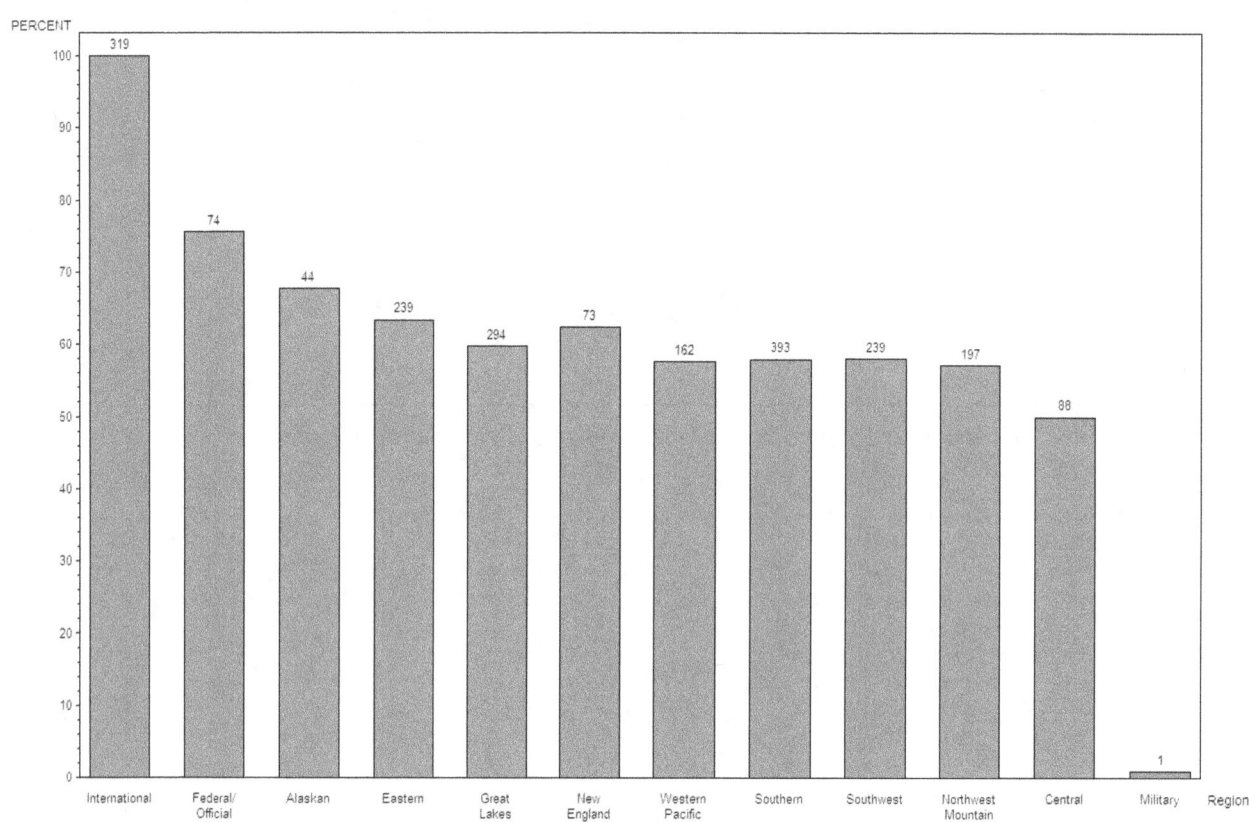

Figure 7. Senior Examiner Status of Active FAA Aviation Medical Examiners by Region

Table 5. Age by Gender of Active FAA Aviation Medical Examiners

			Number	Mean	Median	Standard Deviation	Minimum	Maximum
Overall			3474	59.9	59.6	11.1	28.7	93.4
Gender		Female	268	52.3	52.7	8.9	32.2	82.2
		Male	2843	60.3	59.8	11.2	28.7	93.4
		Not Reported	363	62.8	62.6	9.5	36.0	88.8

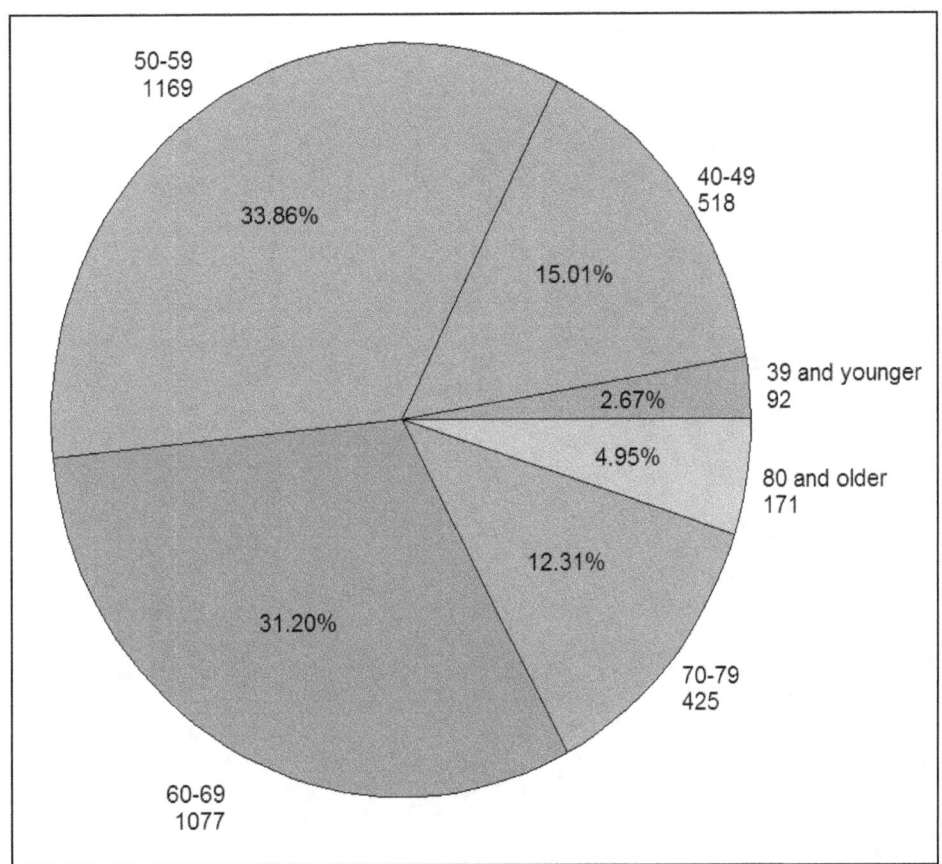

Figure 8. Age Group of Active FAA Aviation Medical Examiners

SECTION II. AIRMAN MEDICAL CERTIFICATION

The Aerospace Medical Certification Division is the central screening facility and repository within the Federal Aviation Administration for the collection, investigation, adjudication, and analysis of medical data.

Activities of the Aerospace Medical Certification Division are presented in this section. Data are presented by calendar year and represent the most recent medical examination data for all active civil aviation airmen in the United States and its territories as of December 31, 2011. Data may slightly fluctuate annually from systematic changes and corrections to the records.

Class issued represents the medical class certificate that was issued at the time of the examination. As of July 24, 2008, if the airman is under 40, first- and second-class certificates are valid for 1 year, and third-class certificates are valid for 5 years. If the airman is 40 and older, first-class certificates are valid for 6 months, second-class for 1 year, and third-class for 2 years. The length of certificate validity varies for those requiring a special issuance.

Effective medical class is determined by class issued, the age of the airman, time since exam, and whether the airman had a time limited certificate. A certificate can be issued as a higher class (i.e. first-class) and become valid as a lower class certificate (i.e. third-class) as the validity period expires for each higher class.

All medical data were abstracted from the most recent medical examinations with the exception of medical conditions. Medical conditions are determined by whether the airman has ever reported the condition on any past or current medical examination. Body mass index (BMI) classifications are as follows: Underweight (less than 18.5), Normal (18.5 to 24.9), Overweight (25 to 29.9), and Obese (greater than or equal to 30).

Table 6. Number of Medical Applications Processed by Year

Year	Number of Applications	Percent Change From Previous Year
2001	454,430	N/A
2002	444,214	-2.2
2003	444,732	0.1
2004	444,250	-0.1
2005	438,415	-1.3
2006	440,269	0.4
2007	452,592	2.8
2008*	425,259	-6.0
2009	397,163	-6.6
2010	394,695	-0.6
2011	400,069	1.4

*Policy change July 24, 2008 lengthened the time of certificate validity for those under 40 years of age.

Table 7. Issued and Effective Medical Class by Region

Region *	First				Second			Third		Total Active Airmen				
	1st Class Certified	Effective Class			2nd Class Certified	Effective Class		3rd Class Certified	Effective Class	Total Airmen Certified	Percent of Total Airmen	Effective Class		
		1	2	3		2	3		3			1	2	3
Alaskan	1,923	1,473	159	291	2,202	1,457	745	4,020	4,020	8,145	1.4	1,473	1,616	5,056
Central	4,816	3,204	506	1,106	5,822	3,559	2,263	13,632	13,632	24,270	4.1	3,204	4,065	17,001
Eastern	18,972	12,926	1,519	4,527	13,517	7,362	6,155	32,817	32,817	65,306	11.0	12,926	8,881	43,499
Great Lakes	26,511	18,104	1,849	6,558	15,378	8,899	6,479	39,789	39,789	81,678	13.7	18,104	10,748	52,826
New England	6,198	4,364	449	1,385	4,089	2,369	1,720	10,825	10,825	21,112	3.6	4,364	2,818	13,930
Northwest-Mountain	18,725	12,700	1,529	4,496	15,315	8,523	6,792	27,840	27,840	61,880	10.4	12,700	10,052	39,128
Southern	42,821	30,157	3,723	8,941	26,186	16,036	10,150	51,388	51,388	120,395	20.3	30,157	19,759	70,479
Southwest	21,251	14,778	1,788	4,685	17,242	10,462	6,780	32,427	32,427	70,920	11.9	14,778	12,250	43,892
Western-Pacific	23,771	15,512	2,173	6,086	19,789	11,566	8,223	43,196	43,196	86,756	14.6	15,512	13,739	57,505
US Total	164,988	113,218	13,695	38,075	119,540	70,233	49,307	255,934	255,934	540,462	90.9	113,218	83,928	343,316
Military	13	0	0	13	2,174	668	1,506	5,396	5,396	7,583	1.3	0	668	6,915
International	24,896	10,226	1,891	12,779	7,936	3,217	4,719	13,437	13,437	46,269	7.8	10,226	5,108	30,935
Total	189,897	123,444	15,586	50,867	129,650	74,118	55,532	274,767	274,767	594,314	100	123,444	89,704	381,166
Percent of Total Certified Airmen	32.0				21.8			46.2			100.0	20.8	15.1	64.1

* 598 airmen with unknown region

Table 8. Issued Medical Class by State of Residence and Gender

| State of Residence * | Issued Medical Class | | | | | | Total Airmen | |
| | First | | Second | | Third | | | |
	Female	Male	Female	Male	Female	Male	Female	Male
Alabama	41	1,146	79	2,465	232	3,840	352	7,451
Alaska	144	1,779	175	2,027	394	3,626	713	7,432
Arizona	382	6,075	271	3,678	612	7,502	1,265	17,255
Arkansas	55	886	40	1,393	152	2,373	247	4,652
California	945	12,677	874	12,381	2,570	28,809	4,389	53,867
Colorado	509	5,787	196	2,809	546	6,006	1,251	14,602
Connecticut	90	1,590	64	915	175	2,505	329	5,010
Delaware	26	361	9	306	43	596	78	1,263
District of Columbia	8	97	9	71	39	291	56	459
Florida	1,092	18,125	666	10,328	1,671	18,442	3,429	46,895
Georgia	357	7,387	194	3,389	481	6,835	1,032	17,611
Hawaii	131	1,218	82	720	77	636	290	2,574
Idaho	36	747	81	1,328	188	2,297	305	4,372
Illinois	437	5,599	209	2,929	537	7,066	1,183	15,594
Indiana	190	2,992	88	1,620	284	4,446	562	9,058
Iowa	34	646	43	1,120	196	3,005	273	4,771
Kansas	60	1,177	90	1,703	281	3,638	431	6,518
Kentucky	126	2,463	62	903	172	2,323	360	5,689
Louisiana	52	1,181	69	1,669	148	2,399	269	5,249
Maine	31	486	41	540	101	1,246	173	2,272
Maryland	95	1,762	135	1,542	348	3,640	578	6,944
Massachusetts	148	1,882	97	1,269	339	3,919	584	7,070
Michigan	299	4,083	146	2,266	469	6,369	914	12,718
Minnesota	266	4,141	154	2,102	334	5,168	754	11,411
Mississippi	52	996	37	981	131	1,903	220	3,880
Missouri	95	2,183	106	1,987	309	4,193	510	8,363
Montana	57	613	79	1,045	163	1,877	299	3,535
Nebraska	29	592	24	749	115	1,895	168	3,236
Nevada	120	2,028	113	1,516	250	2,494	483	6,038
New Hampshire	68	1,304	56	706	97	1,350	221	3,360
New Jersey	157	2,647	107	1,561	294	3,992	558	8,200
New Mexico	26	599	101	1,015	158	1,848	285	3,462
New York	269	4,406	218	2,938	587	7,672	1,074	15,016
North Carolina	227	3,959	134	2,518	433	6,385	794	12,862
North Dakota	38	1,030	36	884	61	1,133	135	3,047
Ohio	257	4,648	167	2,481	502	7,109	926	14,238
Oklahoma	78	1,457	128	2,003	327	4,022	533	7,482
Oregon	121	1,399	196	2,453	373	4,193	690	8,045
Pennsylvania	237	4,492	246	2,986	502	6,866	985	14,344
Rhode Island	27	295	12	164	31	447	70	906
South Carolina	86	1,602	73	1,340	190	3,025	349	5,967
South Dakota	24	301	33	621	59	1,050	116	1,972
Tennessee	210	4,096	155	2,401	312	4,291	677	10,788
Texas	750	16,167	656	10,168	1,532	19,468	2,938	45,803
Utah	159	2,948	149	2,243	160	2,353	468	7,544
Vermont	19	258	15	210	41	574	75	1,042
Virginia	235	3,816	185	2,664	565	6,140	985	12,620
Washington	430	5,635	309	3,988	671	7,893	1,410	17,516
West Virginia	15	278	18	392	76	994	109	1,664
Wisconsin	119	2,087	101	1,541	370	4,832	590	8,460
Wyoming	16	268	30	409	95	1,025	141	1,702
US Territories	49	1,053	44	692	80	1,045	173	2,790
Military	1	12	78	2,096	509	4,887	588	6,995
International	1,440	23,456	388	7,548	916	12,521	2,744	43,525
Total	10,965	178,912	7,868	121,773	20,298	254,454	39,131	555,139

*642 airmen missing state

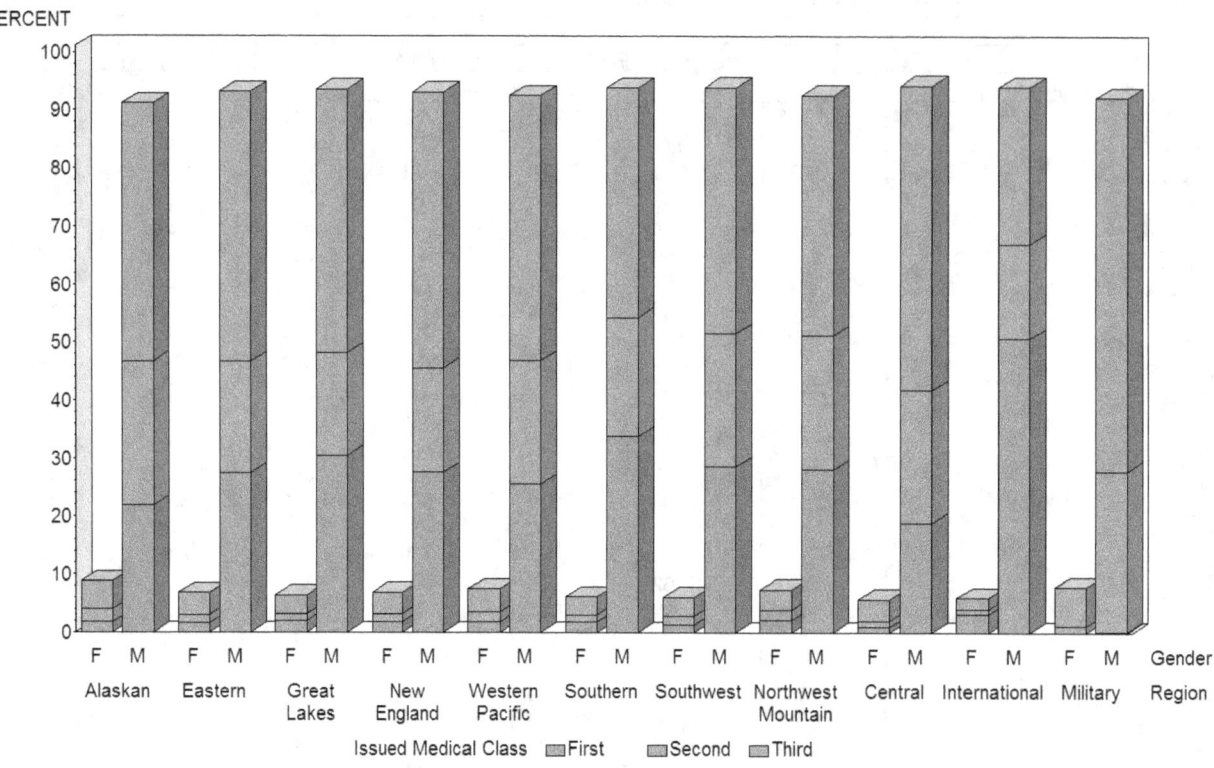

Figure 9. Issued Medical Class by Region and Gender

Table 9. Age as of 12/31/2011 of all Active Airmen by Effective Medical Class

Effective Medical Class	Number of Airmen	Mean	Median	Standard Deviation
First	123,548	43.2	44.2	12.2
Second	89,766	49.1	49.8	13.5
Third	381,598	43.1	41.0	16.5
All Classes	594,912	44.1	43.6	15.4

Table 10. Age Groups of all Active Airmen by Effective Medical Class

Age Group (as of 12/31/2011)	Effective Medical Class Number (Percent)		
	First	Second	Third
16-19	2,673 (2.16)	1,531 (1.71)	10,152 (2.66)
20-24	6,970 (5.64)	3,854 (4.29)	49,287 (12.92)
25-29	11,906 (9.64)	4,882 (5.44)	51,682 (13.54)
30-34	13,765 (11.14)	4,466 (4.98)	38,075 (9.98)
35-39	14,415 (11.67)	5,010 (5.58)	33,747 (8.84)
40-44	14,521 (11.75)	11,596 (12.92)	34,561 (9.06)
45-49	16,921 (13.70)	14,240 (15.86)	26,704 (7.00)
50-54	18,747 (15.17)	13,148 (14.65)	32,169 (8.43)
55-59	14,179 (11.48)	10,845 (12.08)	33,088 (8.67)
60-64	7,590 (6.14)	9,435 (10.51)	28,025 (7.34)
65+	1,861 (1.51)	10,759 (11.99)	44,108 (11.56)
Total	123,548 (20.77)	89,766 (15.09)	381,598 (64.14)

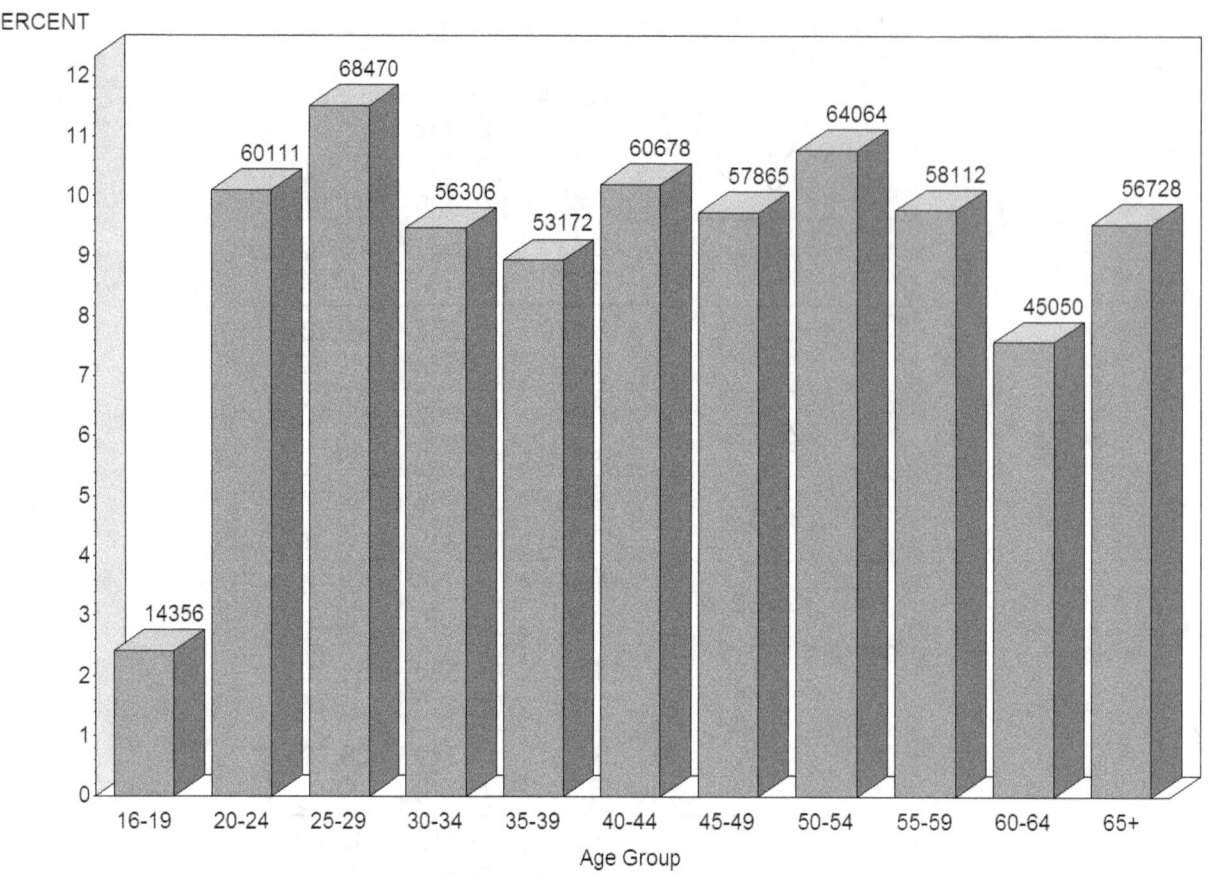

Figure 10. Age Groups as of 12/31/2011 of all Active Airmen

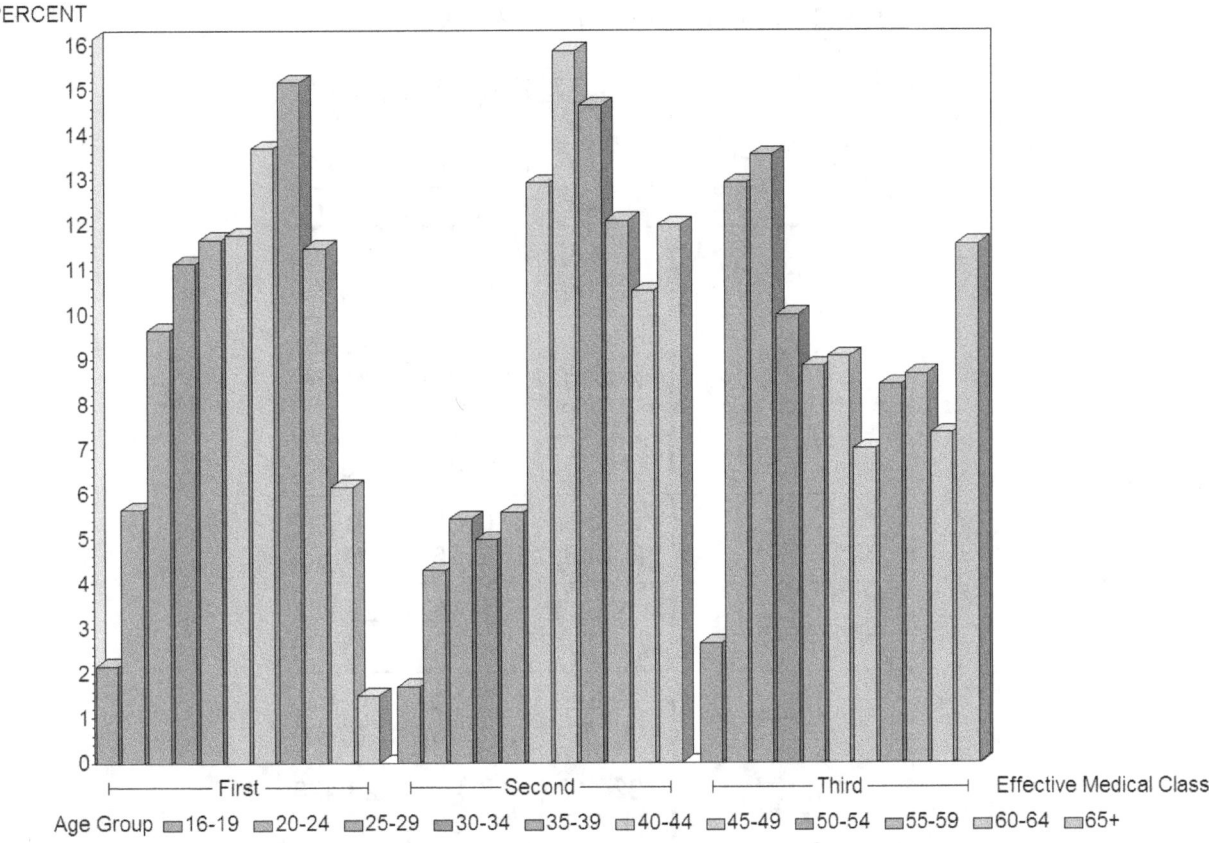

PERCENT

Age Group ▫16-19 ▫20-24 ▫25-29 ▫30-34 ▫35-39 ▫40-44 ▫45-49 ▫50-54 ▫55-59 ▫60-64 ▫65+

Figure 11. Age Groups as of 12/31/2011 by Effective Medical Class for all Active Airmen

Table 11. Age at Exam Summary Statistics for Active Airmen by Issued Medical Class

Issued Medical Class	Number of Airmen	Mean	Median	Standard Deviation
First	190,125	39.8	39.6	13.5
Second	129,740	43.1	43.1	15.8
Third	275,047	44.5	45.5	17.3
All Classes	594,186	42.7	42.7	15.9

Table 12. Age Groups for all Active Airmen by Issued Medical Class

Age Group (at time of exam)	Issued Medical Class Number (Percent)		
	First	Second	Third
16-19	12,665 (6.66)	7,774 (5.99)	18,963 (6.89)
20-24	21,254 (11.18)	13,883 (10.70)	32,137 (11.68)
25-29	22,364 (11.76)	13,550 (10.44)	24,370 (8.86)
30-34	21,071 (11.08)	10,708 (8.25)	20,702 (7.53)
35-39	19,545 (10.28)	12,779 (9.85)	23,951 (8.71)
40-44	19,310 (10.16)	10,672 (8.23)	15,431 (5.61)
45-49	22,419 (11.79)	13,438 (10.36)	23,423 (8.52)
50-54	22,388 (11.78)	13,142 (10.13)	28,865 (10.49)
55-59	16,620 (8.74)	11,498 (8.86)	28,247 (10.27)
60-64	9,615 (5.06)	10,546 (8.13)	23,567 (8.57)
65+	2,874 (1.51)	11,750 (9.06)	35,391 (12.87)
Total	190,125 (31.96)	129,740 (21.81)	275,047 (46.23)

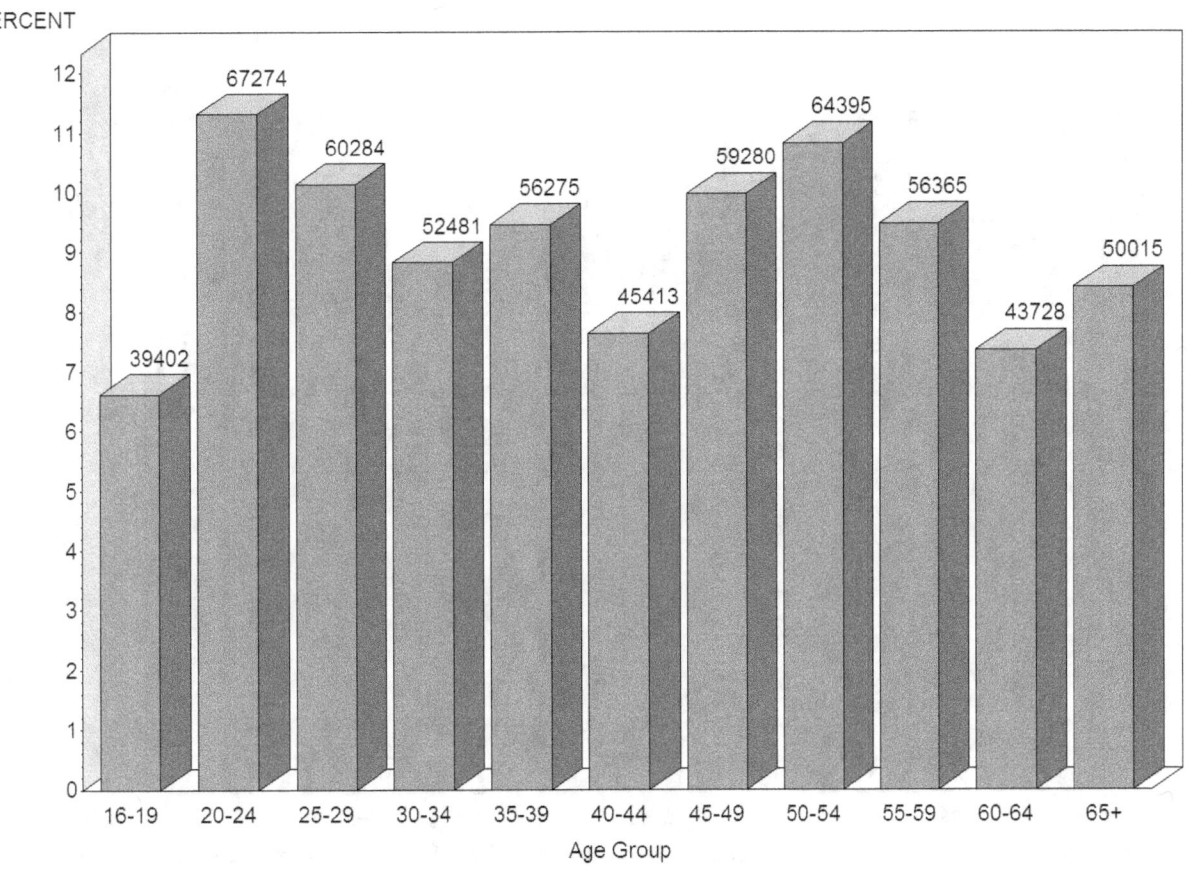

Figure 12. Age Group of all Active Airmen at Time of Exam

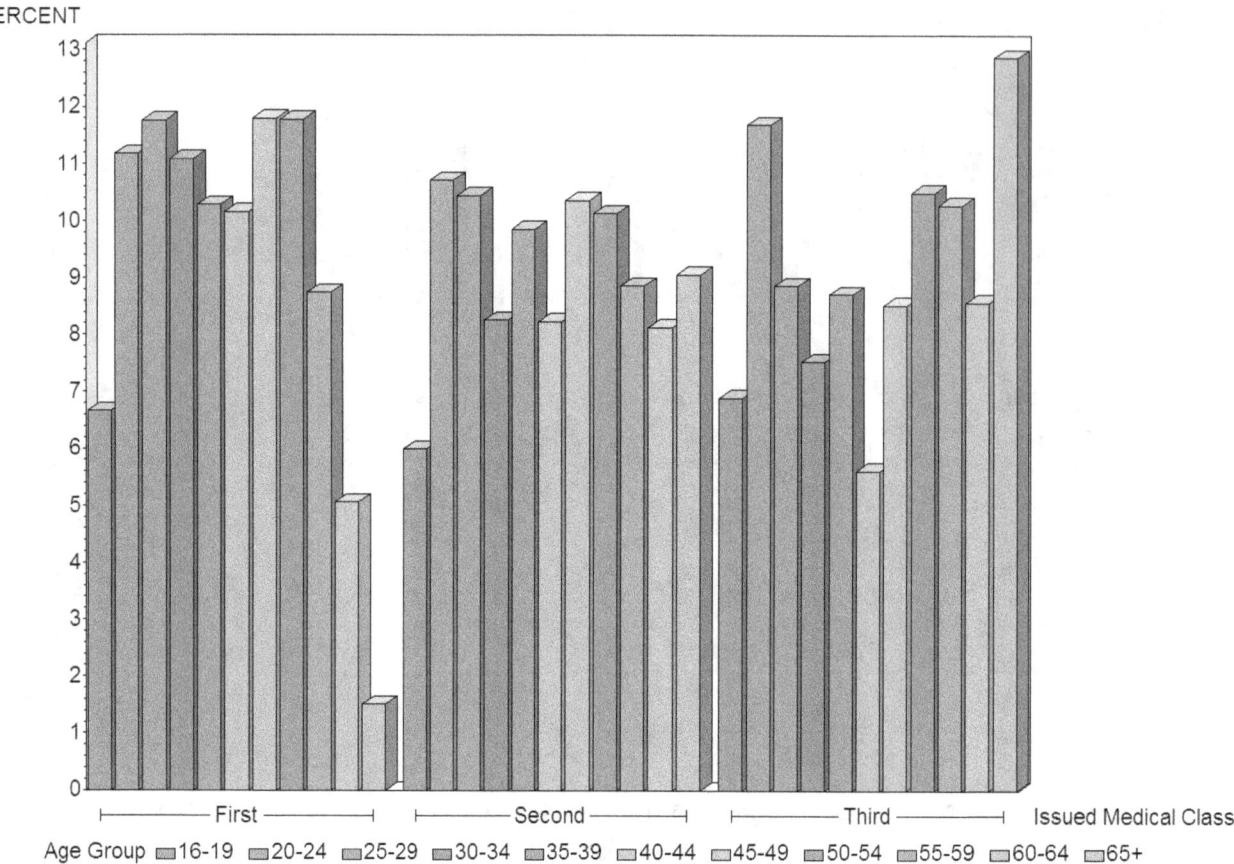

Figure 13. Age Groups by Issued Medical Class for all Active Airmen at Time of Exam

Table 13. Age at Time of Exam by Issued Medical Class and Gender

Age Group	Issued Medical Class						Total Airmen	
	First		Second		Third			
	Female	Male	Female	Male	Female	Male	Female	Male
16-19	1,516	11,149	1,032	6,742	2,787	16,176	5,335	34,067
20-24	1,895	19,359	1,300	12,583	3,349	28,788	6,544	60,730
25-29	1,704	20,660	1,214	12,336	2,366	22,004	5,284	55,000
30-34	1,559	19,512	856	9,852	1,759	18,943	4,174	48,307
35-39	1,227	18,318	858	11,921	1,938	22,013	4,023	52,252
40-44	930	18,380	564	10,108	1,051	14,380	2,545	42,868
45-49	929	21,490	640	12,798	1,437	21,986	3,006	56,274
50-54	712	21,676	560	12,582	1,733	27,132	3,005	61,390
55-59	412	16,208	409	11,089	1,592	26,655	2,413	53,952
60-64	87	9,528	251	10,295	1,101	22,466	1,439	42,289
65+	12	2,862	195	11,555	1,226	34,165	1,433	48,582
Total	10,983	179,142	7,879	121,861	20,339	254,708	39,201	555,711

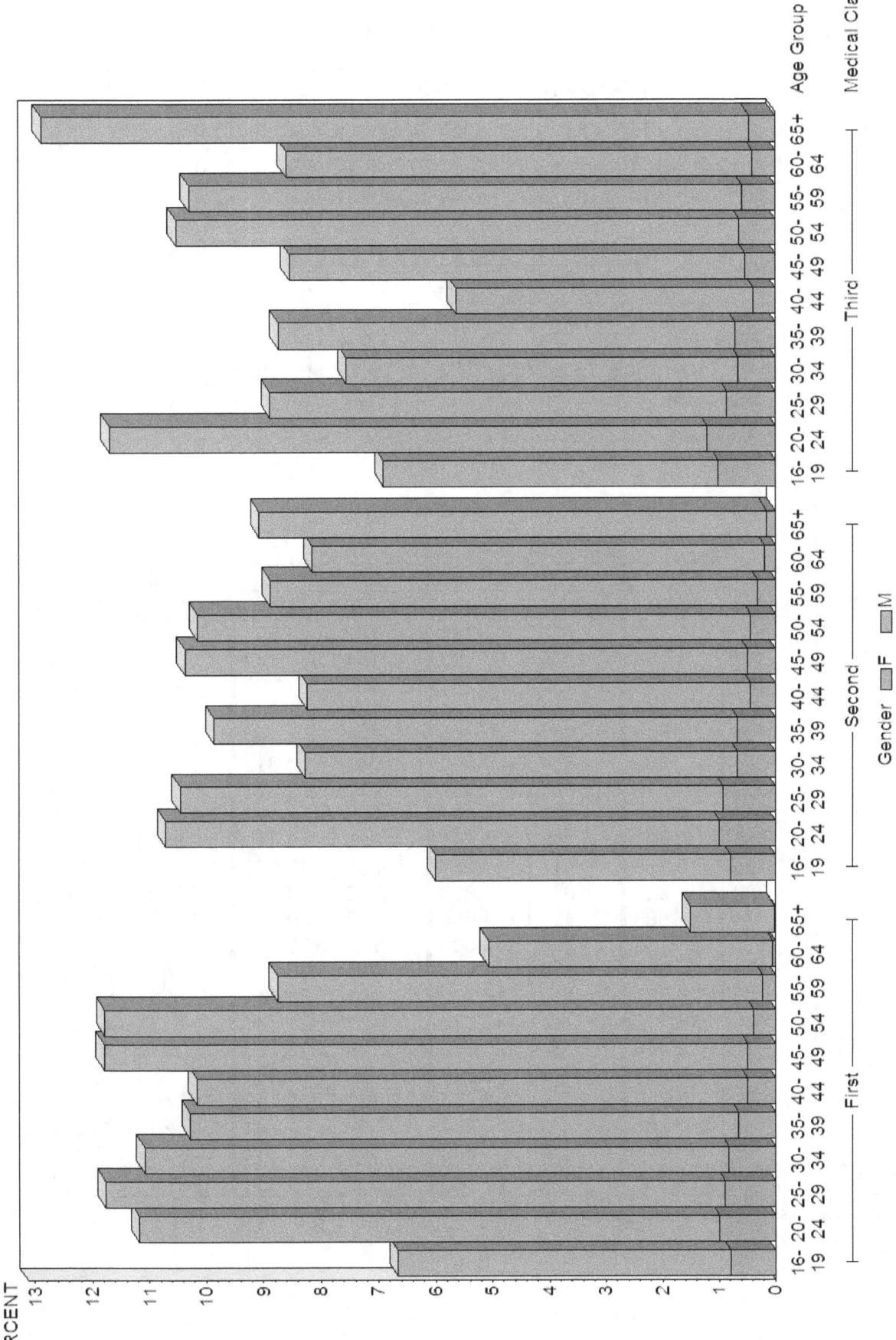

Figure 14. Age Group at Time of Exam by Gender and Issued Medical Class

Table 14. Height (inches) of all Active Airmen by Gender and Issued Medical Class

Issued Medical Class*		Number of Airmen	Mean	Median	Standard Deviation
First	Females	10,983	65.5	65.0	2.8
	Males	179,133	70.6	71.0	2.7
Second	Females	7,879	65.5	65.0	2.9
	Males	121,856	70.5	71.0	2.7
Third	Females	20,337	65.5	65.0	3.0
	Males	254,688	70.5	70.0	2.8
All Classes	Females	39,199	65.5	65.0	2.9
	Males	555,677	70.5	71.0	2.7

*36 airmen missing height

Table 15. Height (inches) by Issued Medical Class and Gender

Height*	Issued Medical Class						Total Airmen	
	First		Second		Third			
	Female	Male	Female	Male	Female	Male	Female	Male
<59	50	175	47	161	160	295	257	631
59	47	58	45	63	111	142	203	263
60	185	98	152	141	466	296	803	535
61	367	114	254	120	745	288	1,366	522
62	769	166	587	156	1,583	399	2,939	721
63	1,055	366	804	303	2,041	818	3,900	1,487
64	1,529	1,216	1,095	852	2,772	2,072	5,396	4,140
65	1,565	2,636	1,083	1,851	2,725	4,124	5,373	8,611
66	1,655	6,128	1,156	4,507	2,835	9,449	5,646	20,084
67	1,325	10,758	917	7,277	2,285	15,678	4,527	33,713
68	989	16,925	657	11,838	1,706	24,839	3,352	53,602
69	624	21,596	439	14,894	1,107	30,335	2,170	66,825
70	398	27,166	291	18,500	751	39,177	1,440	84,843
71	193	24,383	135	16,940	421	35,286	749	76,609
72	122	26,882	116	18,222	291	36,749	529	81,853
73	50	16,012	42	10,388	121	21,536	213	47,936
74	24	12,338	33	7,852	106	16,329	163	36,519
75	12	6,303	13	3,920	58	8,591	83	18,814
76	11	3,740	6	2,415	29	5,155	46	11,310
77	7	1,257	3	867	10	1,783	20	3,907
78+	6	816	4	589	14	1,347	24	2,752
Total	10,983	179,133	7,879	121,856	20,337	254,688	39,199	555,677

*36 airmen missing height and/or gender

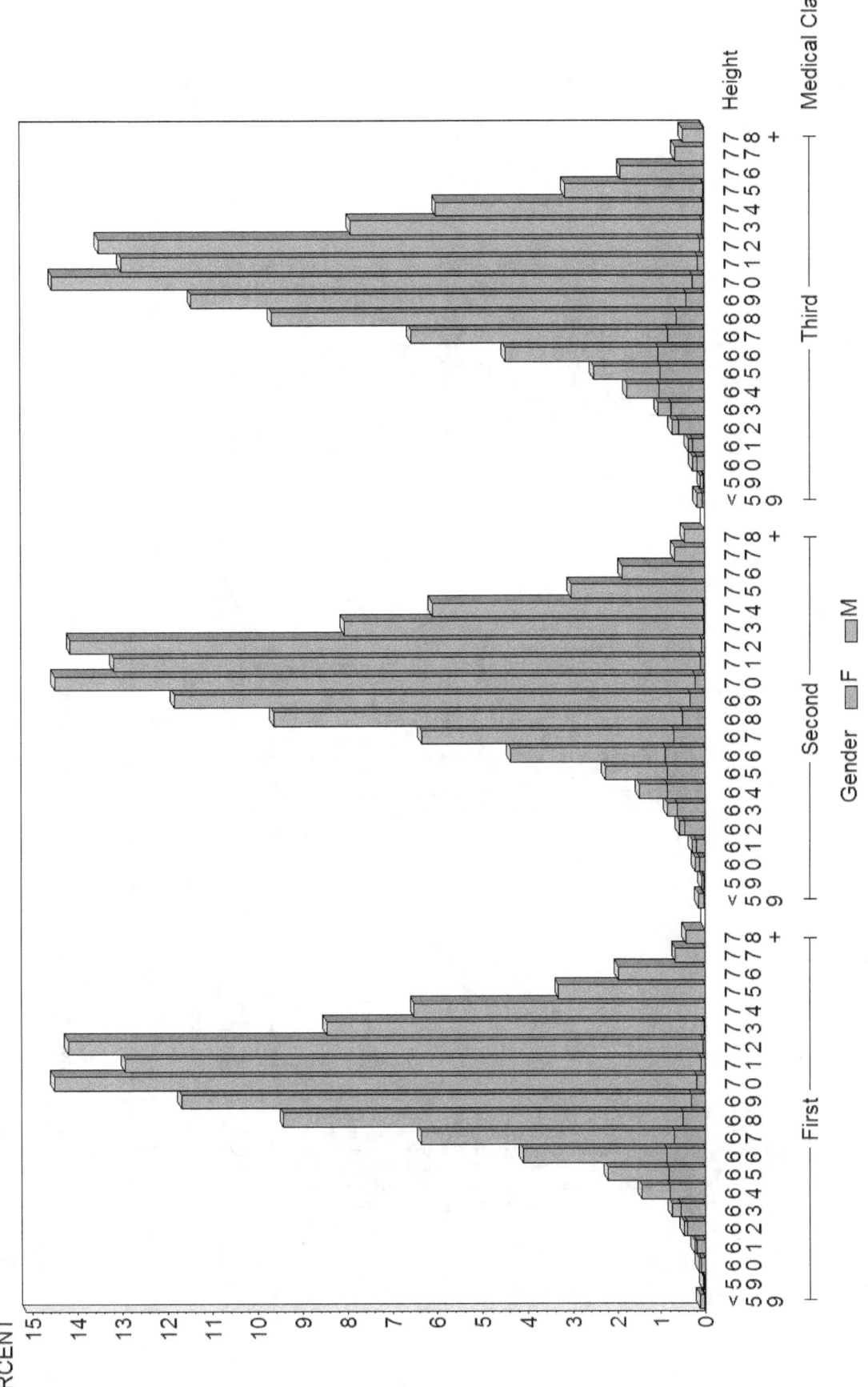

Figure 15. Height (inches) by Gender and Issued Medical Class

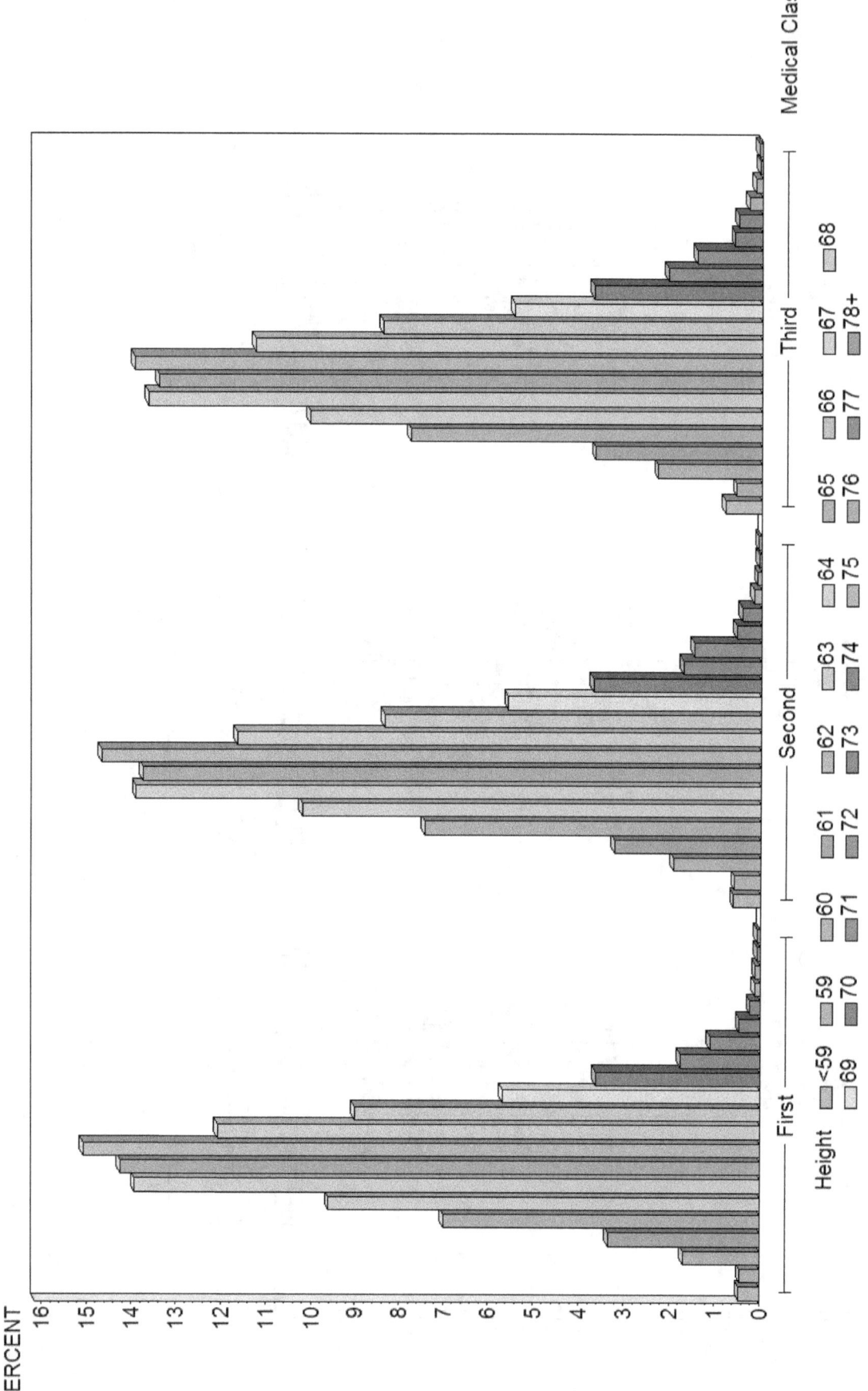

Figure 16. Height (inches) by Issued Medical Class – Females Only

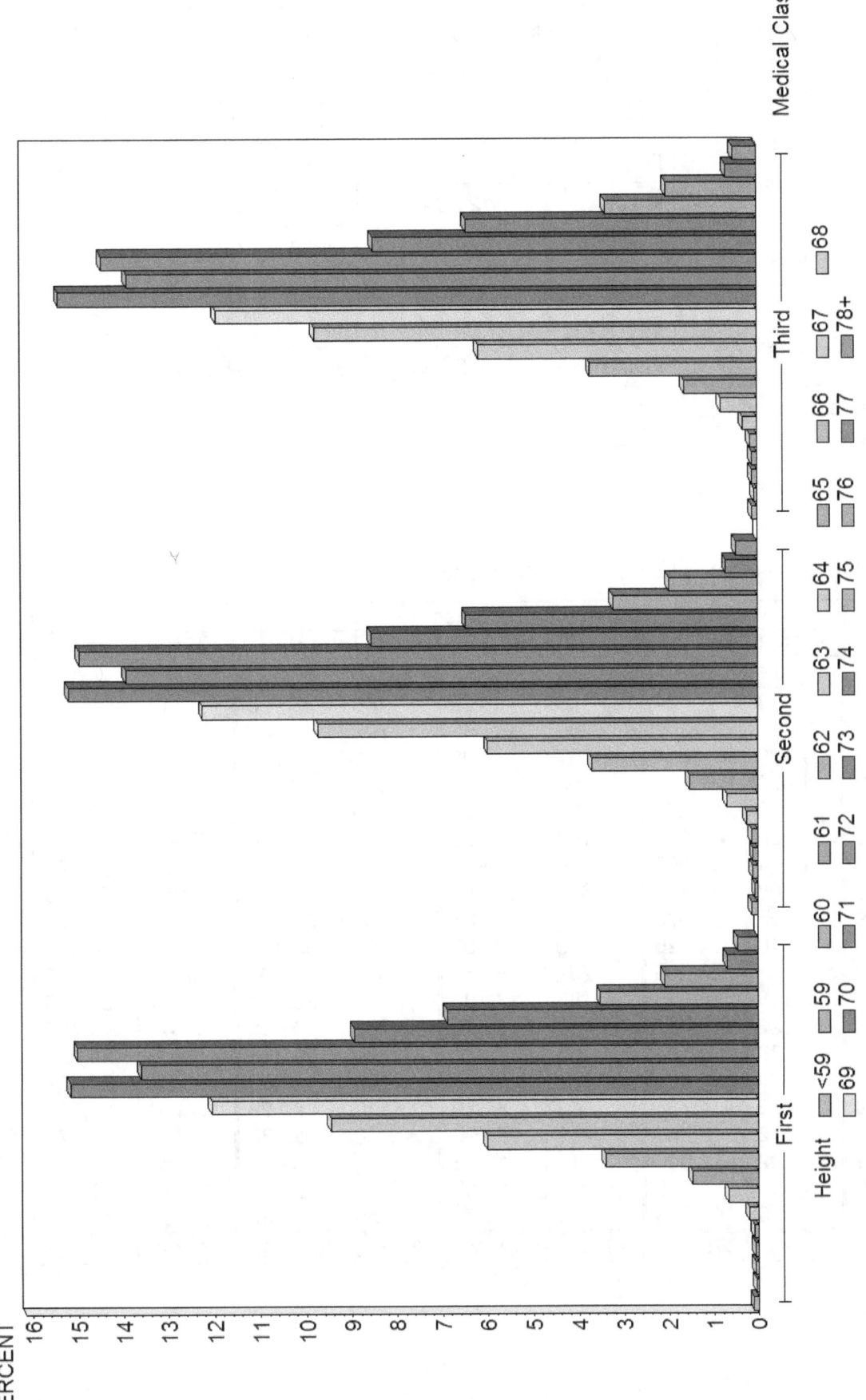

Figure 17. Height (inches) by Issued Medical Class – Males Only

Table 16. Weight (pounds) of all Active Airmen by Gender and Issued Medical Class

Issued Medical Class*		Number of Airmen	Mean	Median	Standard Deviation
First	Females	10,980	144.4	139.0	28.3
	Males	179,126	190.3	187.0	32.8
Second	Females	7,878	149.9	143.0	32.3
	Males	121,846	194.2	190.0	34.0
Third	Females	20,335	148.4	142.0	31.1
	Males	254,683	193.9	190.0	34.5
All Classes	Females	39,193	147.6	141.0	30.7
	Males	555,655	192.8	190.0	33.9

*64 missing weight

Table 17. Weight (pounds) by Issued Medical Class and Gender

Weight*	Issued Medical Class						Total Airmen	
	First		Second		Third			
	Female	Male	Female	Male	Female	Male	Female	Male
<100	113	54	53	29	148	56	314	139
100-109	406	172	268	71	702	166	1,376	409
110-119	1,139	614	687	308	1,851	688	3,677	1,610
120-129	1,829	1,747	1,150	967	3,108	2,239	6,087	4,953
130-139	2,058	4,132	1,297	2,412	3,420	5,106	6,775	11,650
140-149	1,625	7,818	1,183	4,538	3,041	10,086	5,849	22,442
150-159	1,214	13,099	844	7,900	2,277	16,996	4,335	37,995
160-169	808	18,653	644	11,347	1,632	24,335	3,084	54,335
170-179	565	23,073	476	14,463	1,260	30,641	2,301	68,177
180-189	410	24,826	378	16,207	853	33,445	1,641	74,478
190-199	284	22,106	257	14,953	600	30,901	1,141	67,960
200-209	158	18,050	185	13,103	438	26,413	781	57,566
210-219	122	13,726	142	10,358	281	20,698	545	44,782
220-229	80	10,186	96	7,812	230	16,281	406	34,279
230-239	70	7,150	73	5,655	164	11,657	307	24,462
240-249	28	4,728	48	3,879	110	8,128	186	16,735
250-259	22	3,251	31	2,696	76	5,529	129	11,476
260-269	22	2,000	17	1,716	49	3,691	88	7,407
270-279	11	1,348	15	1,159	36	2,635	62	5,142
280+	16	2,393	34	2,273	59	4,992	109	9,658
Total	10,980	179,126	7,878	121,846	20,335	254,683	39,193	555,655

*64 airmen missing weight and/or gender

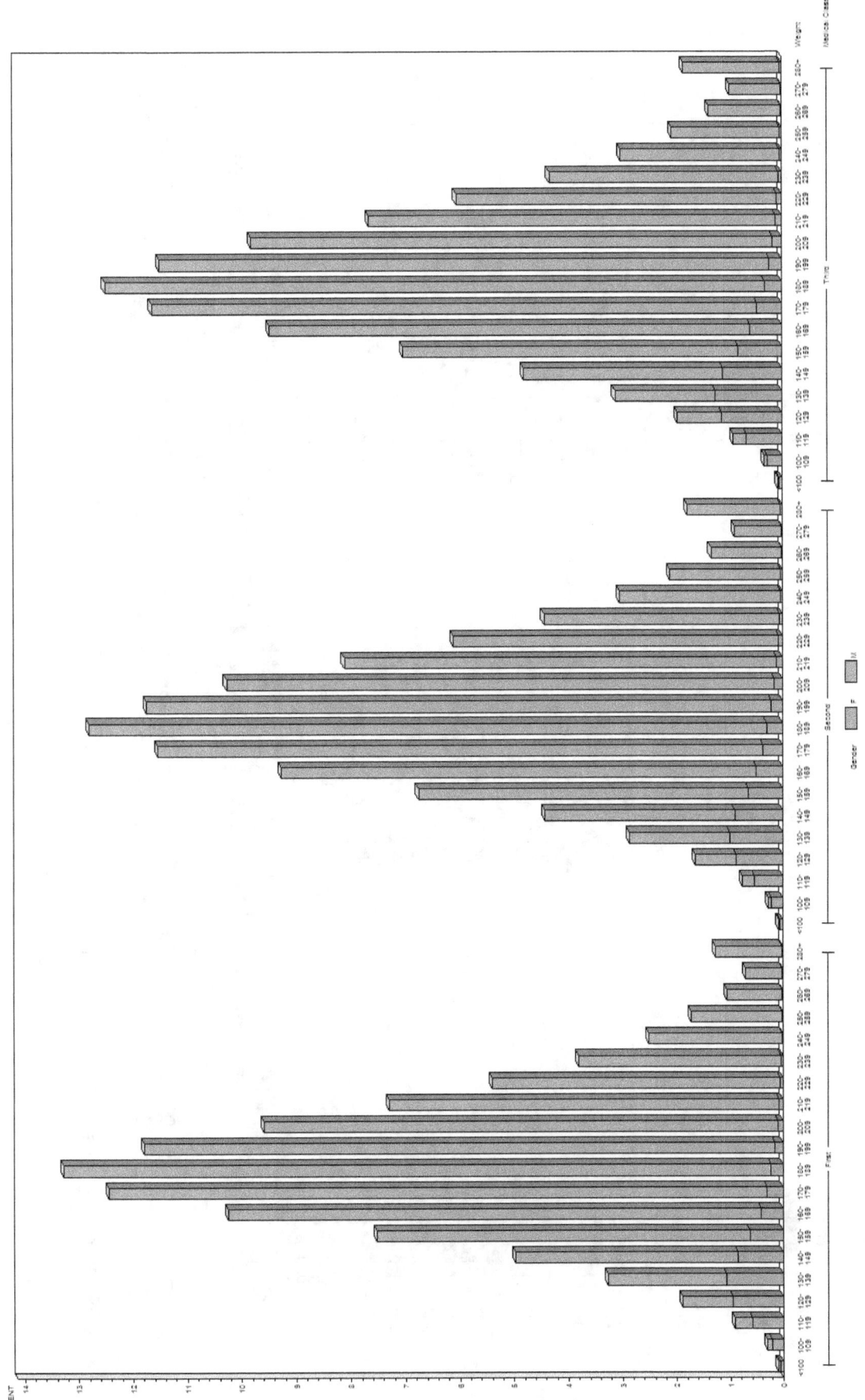

Figure 18. Weight (pounds) by Gender and Issued Medical Class

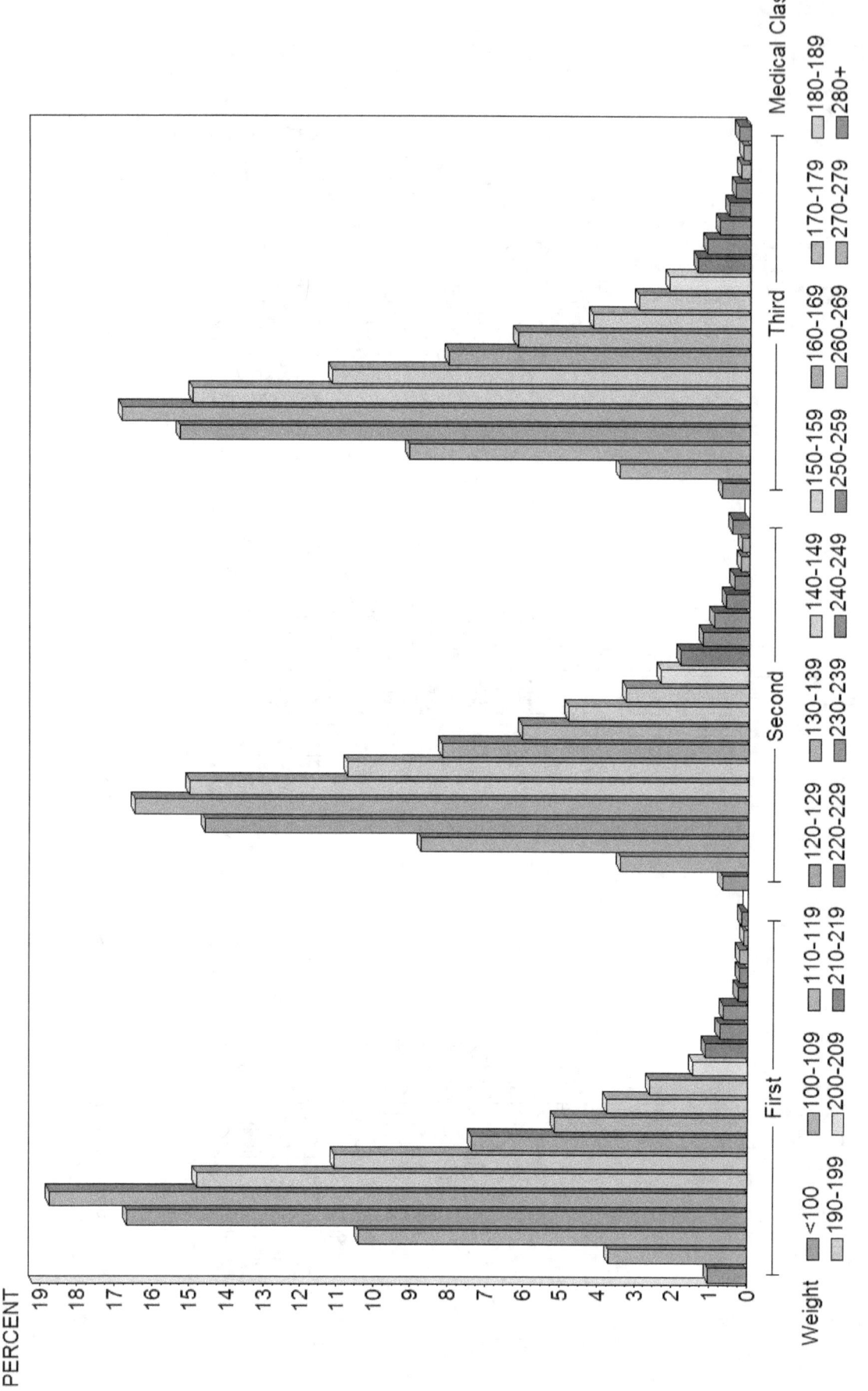

Figure 19. Weight (pounds) by Issued Medical Class – Females Only

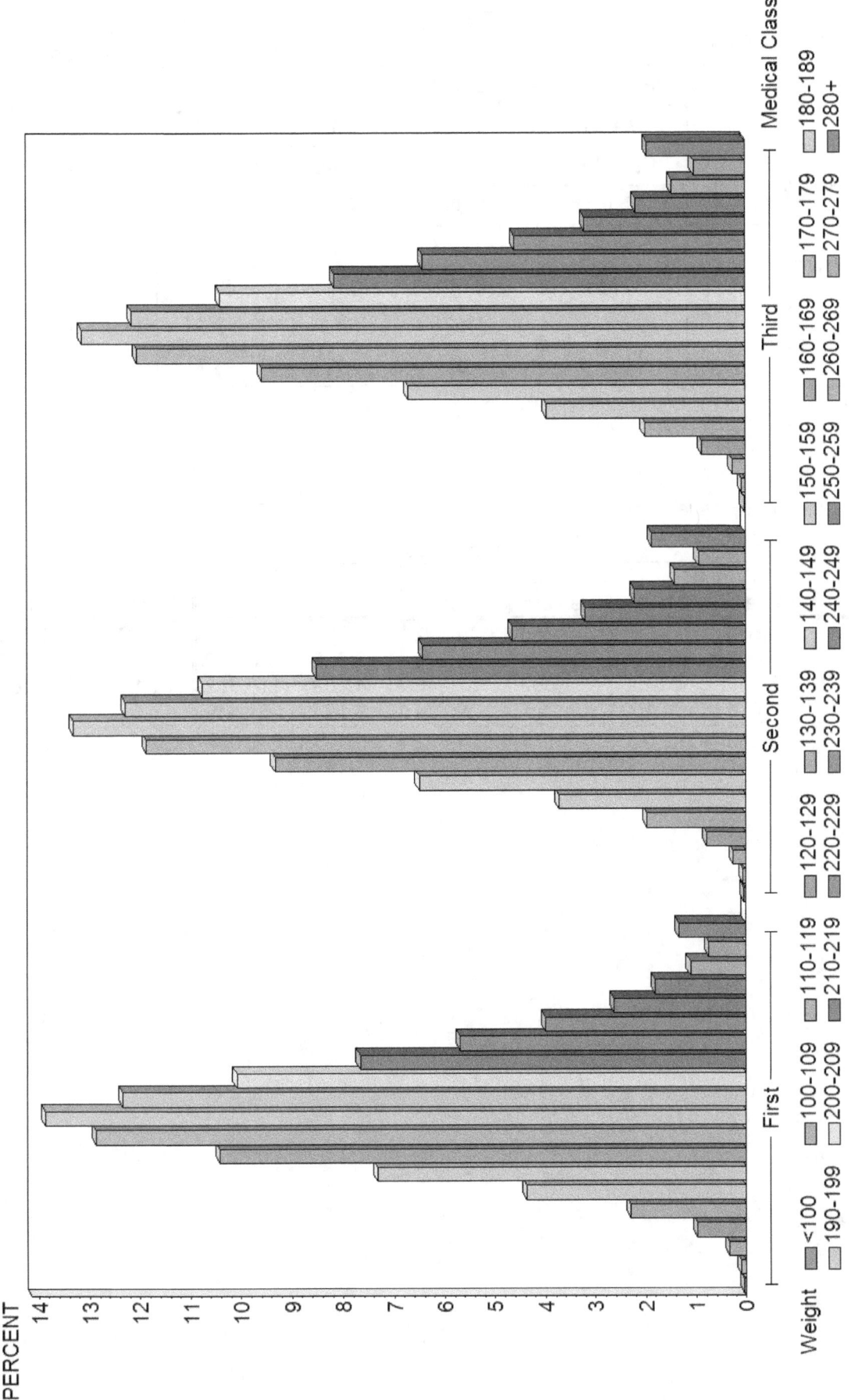

Figure 20. Weight (pounds) by Issued Medical Class – Males Only

Table 18. BMI of all Active Airmen by Gender and Issued Medical Class

Issued Medical Class*		Number of Airmen	Mean	Median	Standard Deviation
First	Females	10,980	23.6	22.7	4.2
	Males	179,120	26.8	26.4	4.2
Second	Females	7,878	24.5	23.5	4.8
	Males	121,842	27.5	27.0	4.4
Third	Females	20,333	24.3	23.3	4.6
	Males	254,665	27.4	26.9	4.5
All Classes	Females	39,191	24.2	23.2	4.6
	Males	555,627	27.2	26.7	4.4

*94 airmen missing BMI

Table 19. BMI Category by Issued Medical Class and Gender

| BMI* | Issued Medical Class | | | | | | | |
| | First | | Second | | Third | | Total Airmen | |
	Female	Male	Female	Male	Female	Male	Female	Male
Underweight	515	1,624	285	812	725	1,814	1,525	4,250
Normal	7,349	59,896	4,734	35,310	12,626	75,710	24,709	170,916
Overweight	2,238	83,450	1,852	56,346	4,789	115,692	8,879	255,488
Obese	878	34,150	1,007	29,374	2,193	61,449	4,078	124,973
Total	10,980	179,120	7,878	121,842	20,333	254,665	39,191	555,627

*94 airmen missing BMI and/or gender

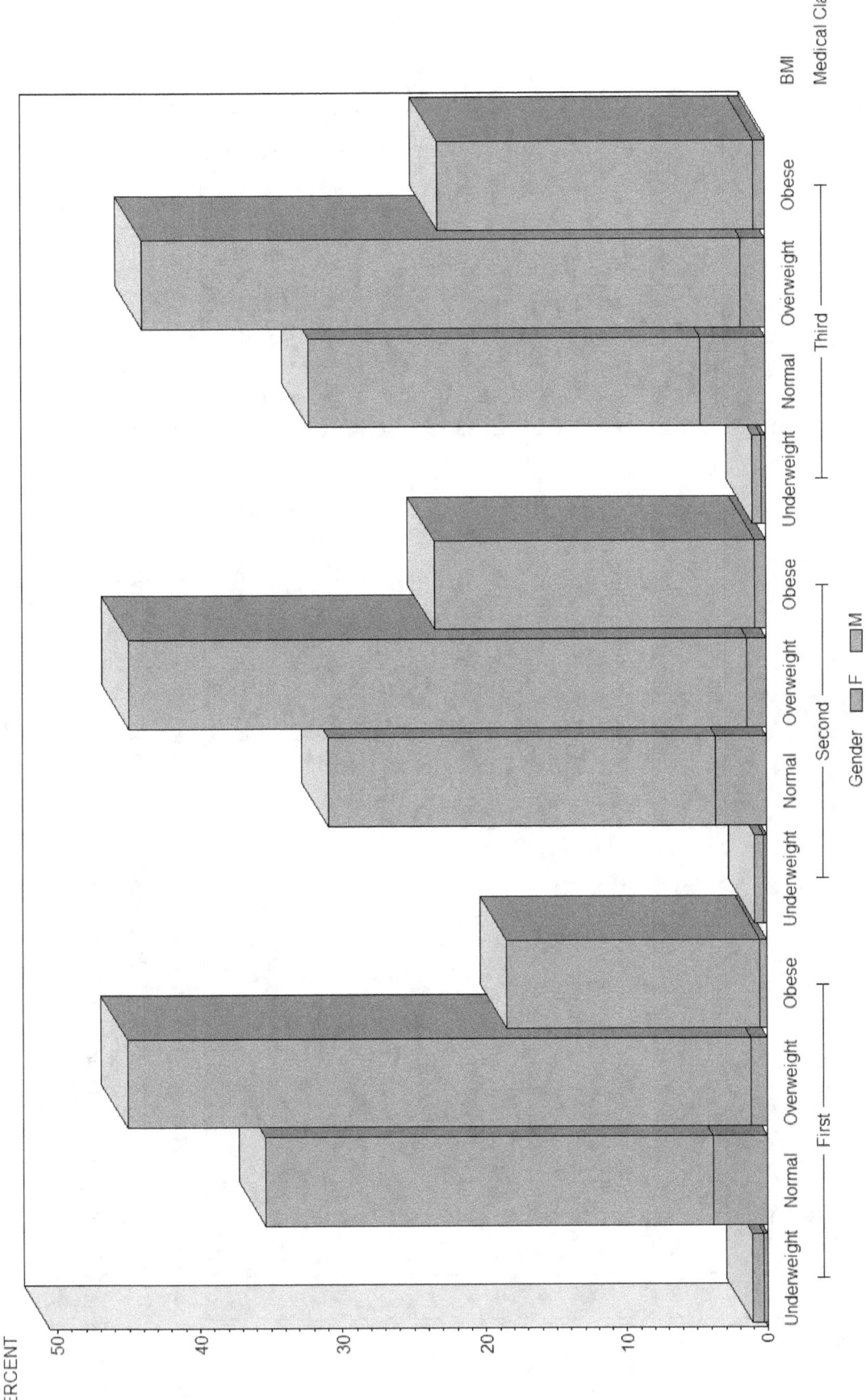

Figure 21. BMI by Gender and Issued Medical Class

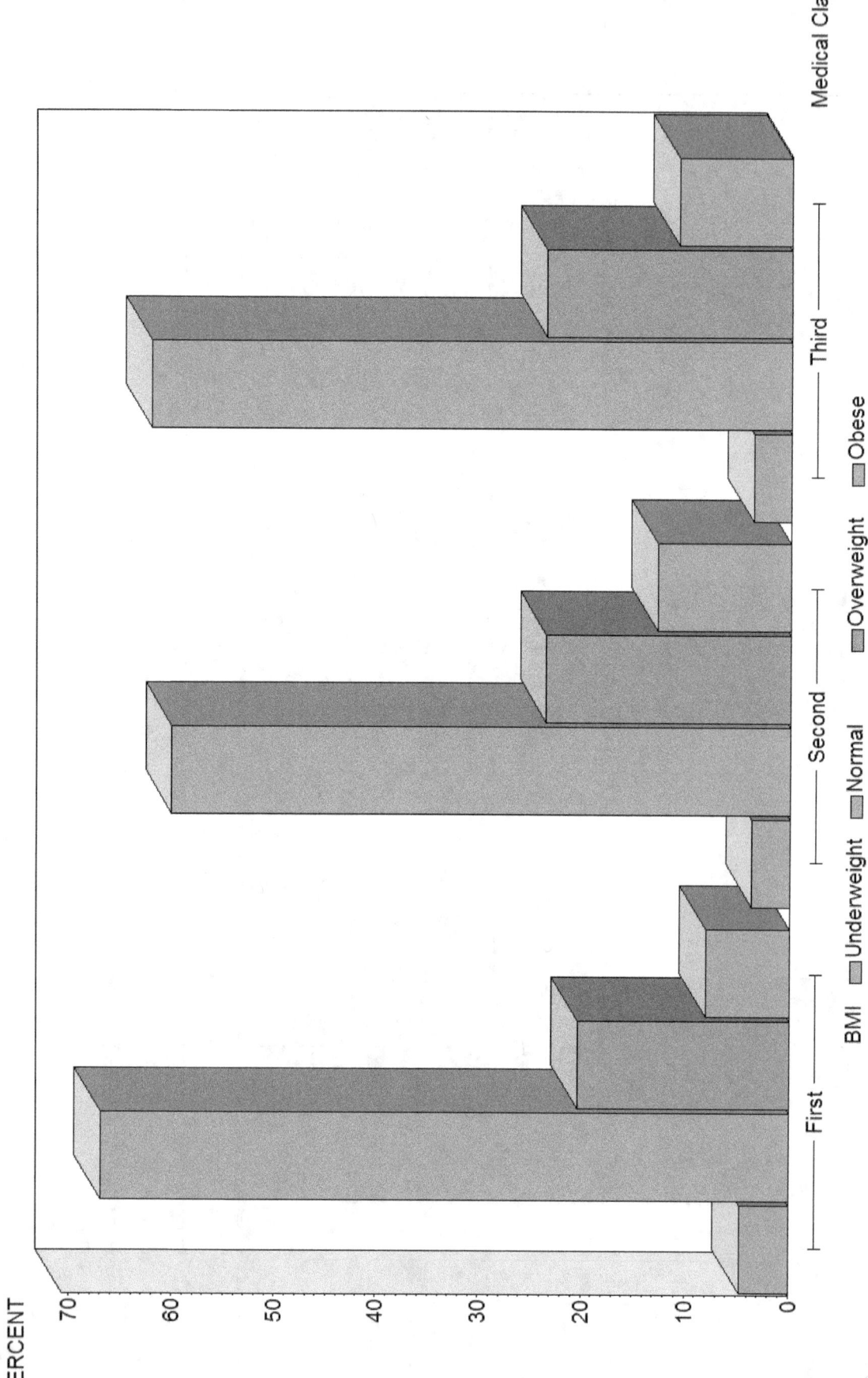

PERCENT

BMI ▪ Underweight ▪ Normal ▪ Overweight ▪ Obese

Figure 22. BMI by Issued Medical Class – Females Only

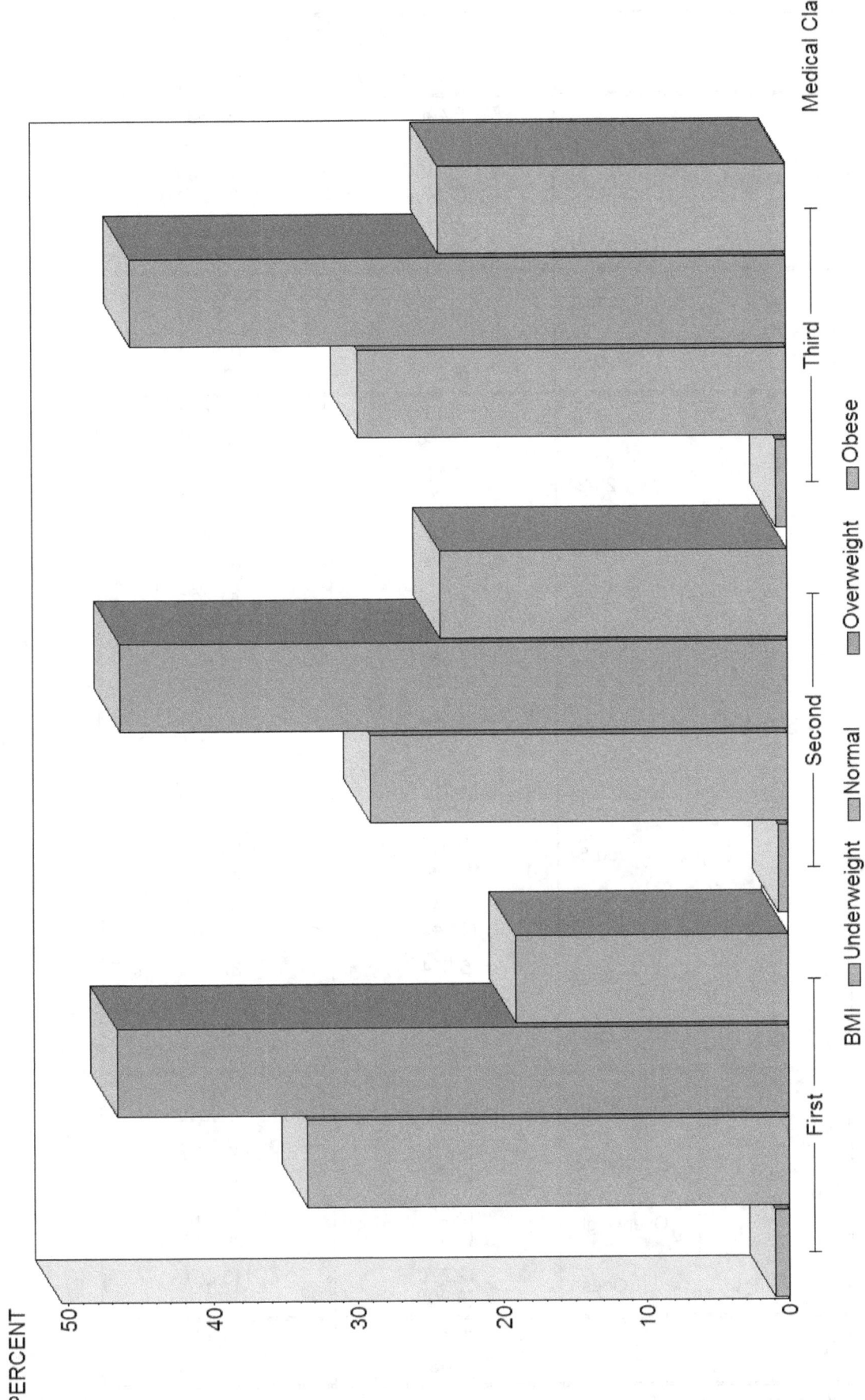

Figure 23. BMI by Issued Medical Class – Males Only

33

Table 20. Special Issuance by Issued Medical Class, Gender, Age, and BMI

		Special Issuance	
		Yes (Percent)	No (Percent)
Class Issued	First	9,440 (4.97)	180,685 (95.03)
	Second	7,240 (5.58)	122,500 (94.42)
	Third	22,781 (8.28)	252,266 (91.72)
Gender	Female	1,610 (4.11)	37,591 (95.89)
	Male	37,851 (6.81)	517,860 (93.19)
Age at Exam	16-19	525 (1.33)	38,877 (98.67)
	20-24	711 (1.06)	66,563 (98.94)
	25-29	866 (1.44)	59,418 (98.56)
	30-34	1,049 (2.00)	51,432 (98.00)
	35-39	1,363 (2.42)	54,912 (97.58)
	40-44	2,054 (4.52)	43,359 (95.48)
	45-49	3,421 (5.77)	55,859 (94.23)
	50-54	5,394 (8.38)	59,001 (91.62)
	55-59	6,443 (11.43)	49,922 (88.57)
	60-64	6,594 (15.08)	37,134 (84.92)
	65+	11,041 (22.08)	38,974 (77.92)
BMI*	Underweight	113 (1.96)	5,662 (93.04)
	Normal	8,316 (4.25)	187,309 (95.75)
	Overweight	18,254 (6.90)	246,113 (93.10)
	Obese	12,770 (9.90)	116,281 (90.10)
Total		39,461 (6.63)	555,451 (93.37)

*94 airmen missing BMI

Percent with Special Issuance

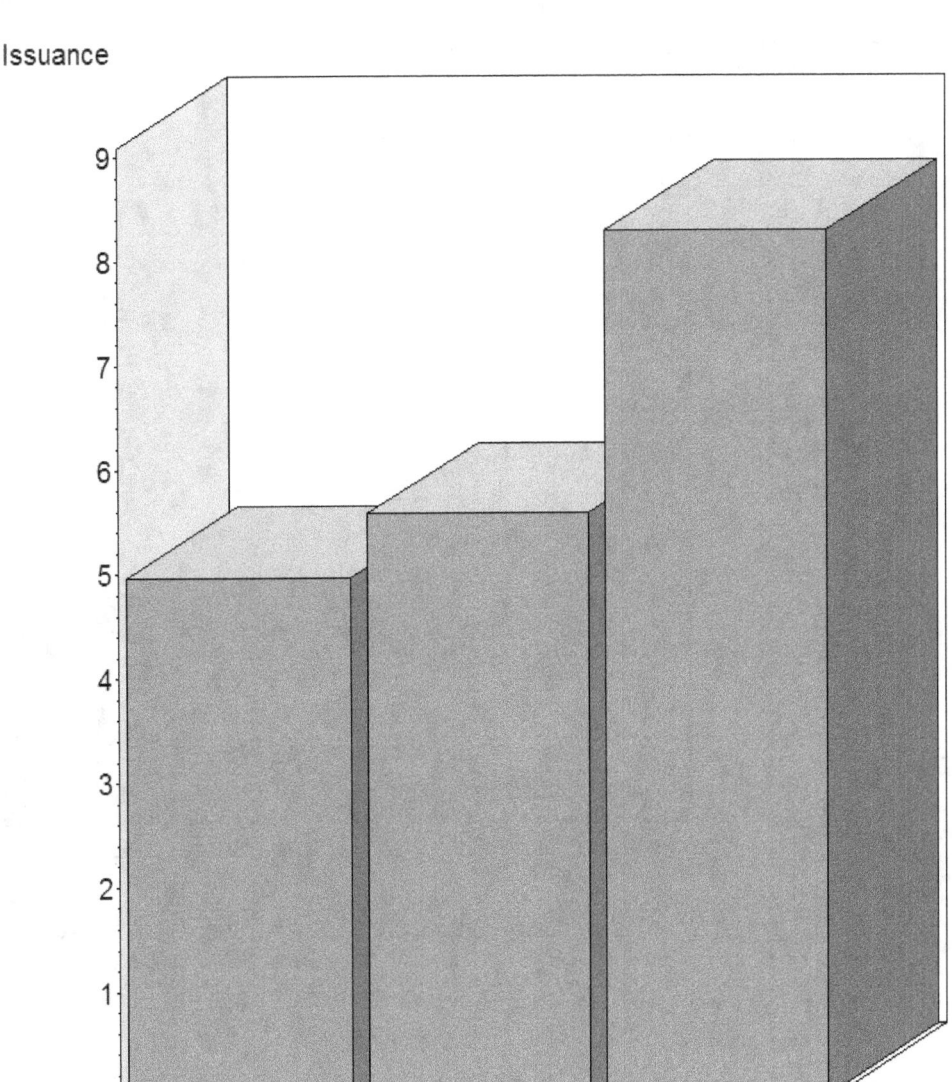

Figure 24. Special Issuance by Issued Medical Class

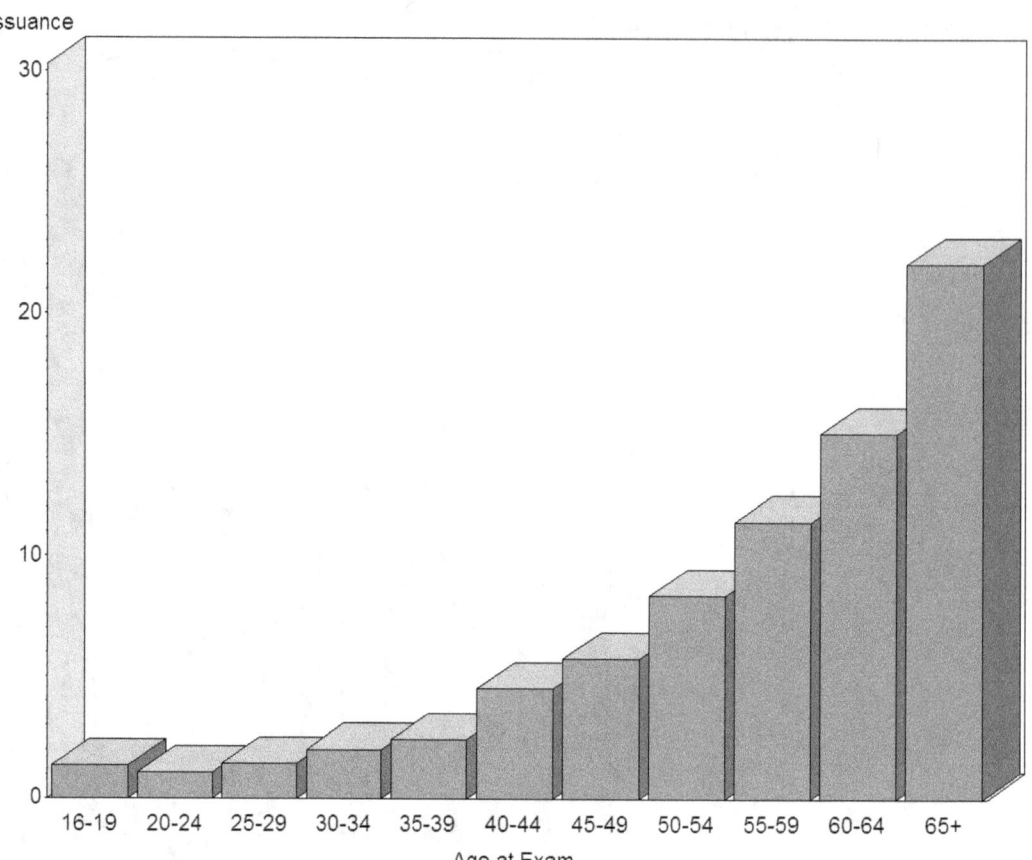

Figure 25. Special Issuance by Age Group at Time of Exam

Percent with Special Issuance

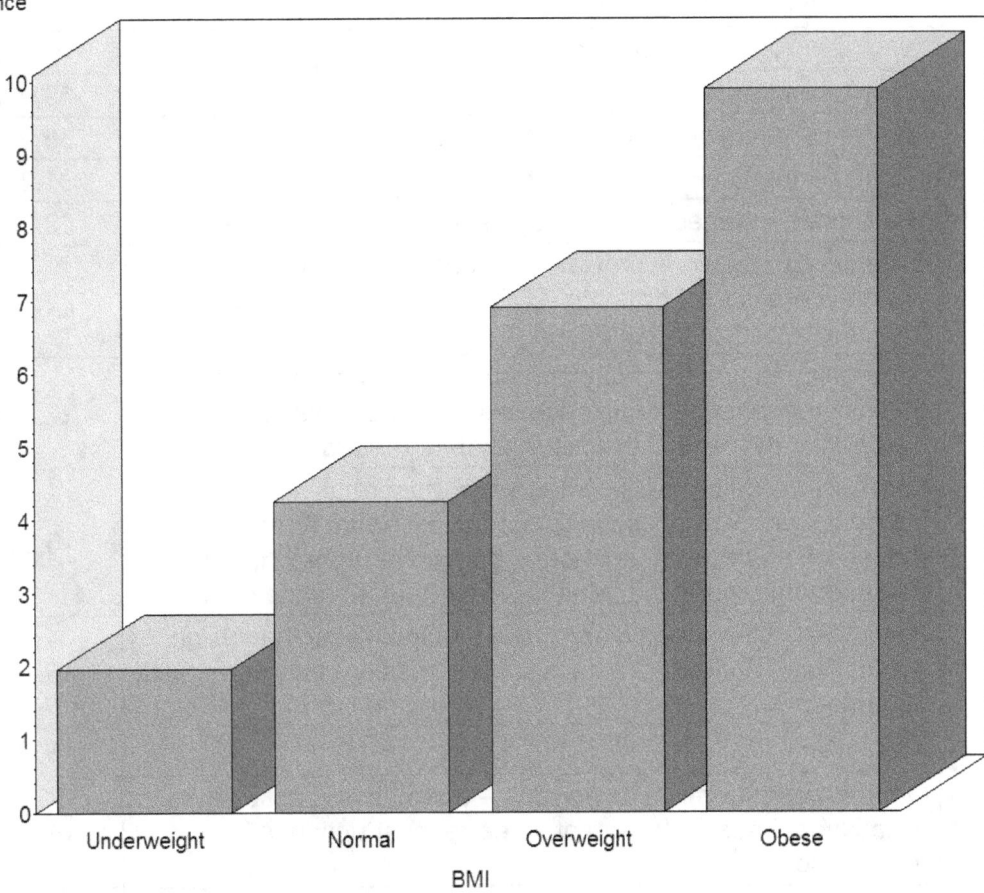

Figure 26. Special Issuance by BMI Category

Table 21. Top 15 Reported Medical Conditions

Pathology Description	Number	Percent
Hypertension with medication	65,902	11.08
Other miscellaneous allergic conditions*	38,938	6.55
Hernias – inguinal, femoral, umbilical, hiatal	31,235	5.25
Urolithiasis – stones or calculus of kidney, ureter, bladder	23,990	4.03
Male genital system – prostatic, varicocele, hydrocele, trans-urethral resection of prostate (TURP), spermatocele, benign prostatic hypertrophy (BPH)	22,558	3.79
Other esophagus, stomach, and duodenal conditions – severe gastritis, esophageal reflux, achalasia, GERD, gastroplasty, dysphagia, dyspepsia, thrombus abdomen aorta#	22,187	3.73
Other skin conditions – includes acne, abnormal pigmentation, vitiligo, psoriasis, keratosis, neurofibroma, (basal cell carcinoma), adenoma, ganglio neuroma, fibroma, fibroadenoma, neuroma, Morton's neuroma, hemangioma‡	15,660	2.63
Ruptured intervertebral disk, nucleus pulposus, spinal fusion, laminectomy and spinal stenosis, compression disc, other back surgeries	15,128	2.54
Hay fever	15,031	2.53
Other lower extremities conditions – operations, fractures, dislocation, knee replacement, knee reconstruction, ACL reconstruction§	14,769	2.48
Asthma	12,777	2.15
Neuroses – hysterical, hysterical-conversion type, hysterical-dissociative type, phobic, neurasthenic, depersonalization, hypochondriacal, adjustment disorder and other neurosis	11,171	1.88
Other general heart pathology (abnormal ECG, open heart surgery, etc.). Wolff-Parkinson-White syndrome, ablation, AV block, right bundle branch block, left bundle branch block†	10,288	1.73
Murmur – includes functional or physiological	10,086	1.70
Traumatic brain injury, concussion, amnesia, coma (30 minutes or more), loss of memory	10,010	1.68

* Excludes hay fever and asthma

Excludes ulcers, gastrectomy, lapband staple bypass, gastric bypass, hernias, esophageal varices

‡ Excludes dermatitis, pilonidal cyst, significant scarring, melanoma, squamous cell carcinoma

§ Excludes deformity of toes, foot, or leg, diseases (synovitis, arthritis, bursitis, osteomyelitis, neoplasms, polymyalgia rheumatica, etc.), rheumatoid arthritis, unstable knee (locked knee, herniated meniscus, no patella)

† Excludes cardiomyopathy, pacemaker, cardiac stents, cardiac angioplasty

Table 22. Medical Conditions by Issued Medical Class

		Issued Medical Class			Total
		First	Second	Third	
Vision	Color vision deficiency	1,557 (0.82)	924 (0.71)	1,784 (0.65)	4,265 (0.72)
	Monocular vision	278 (0.15)	374 (0.29)	1,328 (0.48)	1,980 (0.33)
Transplants	Lung transplant	1 (0.00)	1 (0.00)	3 (0.00)	5 (0.00)
	Heart transplant	0 (0.00)	0 (0.00)	4 (0.00)	4 (0.00)
	Liver transplant	5 (0.00)	5 (0.00)	43 (0.02)	53 (0.01)
	Kidney transplant	35 (0.02)	28 (0.02)	71 (0.03)	134 (0.02)
Cardiac	Myocardial infarction	562 (0.30)	347 (0.27)	2,135 (0.78)	3,044 (0.51)
	Coronary angioplasty with a stent	771 (0.41)	460 (0.35)	3,063 (1.11)	4,294 (0.72)
	Coronary angioplasty procedure	199 (0.10)	153 (0.12)	726 (0.26)	1,078 (0.18)
	Coronary artery bypass surgery	346 (0.18)	243 (0.19)	1,925 (0.70)	2,514 (0.42)
	Implanted pacemaker	62 (0.03)	55 (0.04)	319 (0.12)	436 (0.07)
	Aortic valve conditions*	510 (0.27)	373 (0.29)	1,336 (0.49)	2,219 (0.37)
	Mitral valve conditions[#]	683 (0.36)	462 (0.36)	1,682 (0.61)	2,827 (0.48)
	Hypertension with medication	13,423 (7.06)	13,594 (10.48)	38,885 (14.14)	65,902 (11.08)

Table 22 (continued). Medical Conditions by Issued Medical Class

		Medical Class Issued			Total
		First	Second	Third	
Alcohol and Drugs	Alcohol abuse/dependence	1,820 (0.96)	958 (0.74)	1,710 (0.62)	4,488 (0.75)
	Drug abuse/dependence	711 (0.37)	551 (0.42)	758 (0.28)	2,020 (0.34)
	Alcohol/Drug case monitored	970 (0.51)	73 (0.06)	15 (0.01)	1,058 (0.18)
	Alcohol related offense[‡]	10,115 (5.32)	7,456 (5.75)	13,773 (5.01)	31,344 (5.27)
	Drug related offense/misuse[§]	526 (0.28)	566 (0.44)	930 (0.34)	2,022 (0.34)
Other conditions of interest	Sleep apnea	1,541 (0.81)	1,255 (0.97)	2,955 (1.07)	5,751 (0.97)
	Applied for SSRI use	41 (0.02)	32 (0.02)	148 (0.05)	221 (0.04)
	SSRI special issuance	19 (0.01)	5 (0.00)	41 (0.01)	65 (0.01)
	Diabetes[†]	1,015 (0.53)	1,375 (1.06)	4,486 (1.63)	6,876 (1.16)

* Includes aortic valvular disease, aortic stenosis, aortic regurgitation, aortic insufficiency, bicuspid aortic valve, also replacement, ruptured aorta or lacerated, aortic bruit

[#] Includes mitral valve disease, mitral stenosis, mitral regurgitation, mitral insufficiency. Does not include valve replacement.

[‡] Includes DUI, DWI, public intox, wet/reckless, .04-.09 blood alcohol

[§] Includes drug offenses and positive drug test other than Drug Industry Program (Failed Drug Testing)

[†] Controlled by hypoglycemic drugs or insulin